The Complete Guide to Taking Tests

THE COMPLETE GUIDE TO TAKING TESTS #6

Bernard Feder

Prentice-Hall, Inc., Englewood Cliffs, New Jersey

The Complete Guide to Taking Tests
by Bernard Feder
Copyright ©1979 by Bernard Feder

Printed in the United States of America
Prentice-Hall International, Inc., London/Prentice-Hall of Australia, Pty. Ltd., Sydney/Prentice-Hall of Canada, Ltd., Toronto/Prentice-Hall of India Private Ltd., New Delhi/Prentice-Hall of Japan, Inc., Tokyo/Prentice-Hall of Southeast Asia Pte. Ltd., Singapore/Whitehall Books Limited, Wellington, New Zealand
10 9 8 7 6 5 4 3 2 1

Library of Congress Cataloging in Publication Data
Feder, Bernard.
    The complete guide to taking tests.
    Includes index.
    1. Examinations—United States—Handbooks, manuals, etc. 2. Scholastic aptitude test—Handbooks, manuals, etc.   I. Title.
    LB3051.F4   371.2'6   78-15296
    ISBN 0-13-160754-5
    ISBN 0-13-160747-2 pbk.

Acknowledgements

Thanks are extended to *Human Behavior* magazine for permission to use sections of my article, "How to Pass Without Actually Cheating," which was published in the June 1977 issue.

I am obligated to those students, teachers, guidance counselors, and psychometricians who gave of their time, their knowledge, and the fruits of their experience in the preparation of this book.

Acknowledgement is made to the American College Testing Program for permission to use sample materials from the 1977–78 edition of *Taking the ACT Assessment*, and to the Psychological Corporation for the materials from which some of the data in Chapter 4 were adapted.

Mention should be made of Dr. W. James Popham of UCLA, with whom I have had only brief personal contact, limited to the number of conversations one can have during a crowded symposium weekend and the views that any two panelists can exchange during an hour's formal discussion. Despite the brevity of our conversations, his views on criterion-referenced testing have strongly influenced my own.

A particularly grateful acknowledgement is made to my friend and colleague, Dr. John W. French, dean of graduate studies at the University of Sarasota. Dr. French had coordinated College Board research at the Educational

Testing Service for several years, and had conducted many coaching studies for ETS. He gave freely of his wealth of knowledge, both in written critiques of sections of this book and in innumerable conversations. I am indebted to Dr. French for his time and expertise, and I fear I have distressed him sorely by my irreverent view of tests, testing, and test-making. His failure to dissuade me from my rather iconoclastic inclinations must be ascribed to my own deep seated impiety, rather than to any lack of effort on his part. Needless to say, the view of tests and testing that emerges in this book does not in any way reflect his own.

Contents

1.
Test-Taking:
A Major Survival Skill

Despite our claim to a tradition of rugged individualism, Americans are probably the most tested, measured, sorted, and classified people who have ever lived on the face of the earth. In the United States today, test-taking has become a major survival skill. Says psychologist Robert Williams, himself a near-casualty of testing (in high school he came within 3 IQ points of being placed in a special education track and was advised to take up bricklaying): "The testing industry has become this country's political and economic gatekeeper. Directly or indirectly, it participates in *controlling* who goes to college, who gets the better jobs, and in short who gets the power."

For about one-third of our population—the third that attends school, from kindergarten through doctoral orals—the testing programs are obvious. Classroom tests are turnstiles to promotion and to degrees. Also, presumably on a more "scientific" level, standardized tests are used to ascertain aptitudes, predict school success, measure attitudes and learning, and open—and shut—doors to further schooling. In fact, there is a current trend toward using standardized "readiness" tests to guard the doors to the kindergarten!

The ability to perform well on tests is not only an educational accomplishment, but a social and psychological one as well. The successful test-taker is praised by teachers and parents and esteemed by classmates. He or she builds a

1

positive self-image and a foundation of confidence that help to shape the future. Conversely, failure to do well feeds upon itself. For young children, school and society are almost synonymous. Humiliation in the classroom follows the failure home and into the playground and the street. The social pressure of the classroom spills into the home and the community.

And the distribution of reward and failure—often described as "preparation for life"—operates within artificially narrow limits. In contrast with life outside of school, success in school focuses on academic achievement. Characteristics that are highly prized outside of school—good looks, charm, a sense of humor, a high level of energy, creativity, courage, physical prowess, grace, mechanical ability, esthetic sensitivity, independence of thought and action—are discounted in the restricted calculation of school success. The measure of school achievement is calculated, by and large, by the child's ability to do well on tests.

Tests don't only measure and reflect school achievement, however; they play a significant role in shaping it. In 1964, Robert Rosenthal of Harvard and Lenore Jacobson of the South San Francisco School District gave all the children in a California elementary school an intelligence test. Twenty percent of the children were selected at random—but teachers were told that test results had identified these students as "spurters," who would show marked gains in intellectual achievement during the school year. The next year the whole school population was retested and—you guessed it—the experimental group showed an impressive gain over the rest of the student body, especially in the early grades. Moreover, the teachers rated the members of the experimental group higher in such nonacademic traits as cooperativeness, interest, and social adjustment. Rosenthal and Jacobson concluded that teacher expectations became a "self-fulfilling prophecy."

The concept of the self-fulfilling prophecy in school has fascinating implications when we consider that virtually all teachers from grade one through high school have access to students' academic records, including IQ and achievement test scores—and the vast majority examine these records. Most teachers have already formed a set of expectations about their students even before they meet their new classes. Furthermore, numerous studies reveal the unbounded confidence most teachers have in standardized tests. This uncritical confidence may be due to the abysmal ignorance of so many teachers about testing. Surveys reveal that the majority of teachers have never received formal instruction in measurement, statistics, or test construction. College and university teachers—who jealously guard the gates to their own disciplines against uncredentialed interlopers—generally assume that they are quite competent to measure, judge, and grade other people's children even when they haven't the haziest notion of such basic testing concepts as *standard error* and haven't the foggiest idea of how to establish the validity or reliability of their own tests.

Tests have, in effect, become the "hidden curriculum" in schools. They communicate what teachers think is worth testing and determine what learners think is worth learning. (Picture a class of note-takers when the teacher announces that "this won't be on the test"!) So students learn to ignore the rhetoric about professed objectives and focus on the real curriculum: test-passing. But teachers as

2

well as students have become casualties of the test-as-curriculum. In this age of "educational accountability," generally based on mass achievement testing, increasing numbers of teachers are themselves evaluated by the scores of their children, although the children bring with them a multitude of variable differences over which neither the schools nor the teachers have much control. Is it any wonder that in many districts teachers have learned that the survival curriculum is teaching-to-the-test? Standardized test critic Banesh Hoffman notes: "The accountability movement . . . has led teachers' organizations to protest—even though, I must add, they did not protest anything like as strongly when only the students were being evaluated by the tests."

Since testing is the primary method for evaluating student achievement and student worth, it would seem reasonable to expect that most school tests would be directly related to the objectives that the school programs profess. But anyone who relies on such expectations is doomed to disappointment. A survey described in the late 1960's in *Social Education,* the journal of the National Council for the Social Studies, is revealing. Richard E. Gross, then NCSS president, and Dwight W. Allen of Stanford University reported results that present a depressing picture of testing in that subject. On the basis of responses from 600 randomly selected members of the organization, presumably among the more enlightened and interested teachers of social studies throughout the country, the investigators came up with a dismal list of 14 conclusions. Among them: teachers frequently fail to relate their assessment practices to the aims they claim for their offerings; teachers are often inconsistent in their conception of evaluation; they place a great amount of blind faith in the indirect accomplishment of their objectives; they have a low level of statistical sophistication; they tend to use testing and grading as coercive weapons; and very few teachers perceive the educational, rather than the grading, functions of a testing program.

But myths have a tendency to persist. School administrators, counselors, teachers, students, and parents are all caught up in a massive pretense that tests really do measure what students have learned about a subject and so, of course, it isn't necessary to teach students to take tests. Deep down, teachers recognize that testmanship has little to do with real understanding, or even with real knowledge. In his book *How Children Fail,* John Holt asks, "What would happen at Harvard or Yale if a prof gave a surprise test in March on work covered in October?" Everyone knows what would happen, Holt answers, and that's why they don't do it. That is also why teachers announce tests in advance, why they provide hints on the types of questions to be asked and the content to be covered. That's why they advise their better students not to think too much about hidden meanings in questions. And that's why students cram for tests. Everyone involved knows quite well that the rules generally call for retention of data, which is often only dimly perceived or understood, until the date of the exam. After that, there comes into operation the "vaccination theory of education" (a term coined by Neil Postman and Charles Weingartner in their *Teaching as a Subversive Activity*). Once a student has "had" a course and passed the exam, he or she is usually immune and need not take the course again or demonstrate that any lasting learning has been gained.

It must be admitted that the system does provide a sense of certainty in an uncertain world. It insulates teachers, parents, and students from the realization that there *is* no foolproof way to measure what has actually been learned. Grades are charms that comfort the uncertain and guide the perplexed. Many teachers and administrators have such unquestioning faith in the precision of test scores that they average them to several decimal places in ascertaining grades (although test experts point out that no two tests, even good ones, are interchangeable). And grades themselves, in many schools, are themselves averaged to fantastic degrees of precision in identifying award recipients and valedictorians.

Dr. Henry Dyer, one of the nation's foremost authorities on testing, thinks that teachers must be educated to be less certain, and more flexible, in using tests. Central to the act of teaching, he wrote in *The Teachers College Record:*

> . . . is the nagging question: "Did it work?" . . . Of course [the teacher] can never know for certain whether her strategy is on the right track, since the instruments and techniques on which she has to depend for checking her hunches and hypotheses about procedure are never wholly reliable or relevant. In most cases, I believe, the realization of uncertainty is achieved only after the cold steel of such ideas as sampling error, the variability of human behavior, and the fallibility of casual observation and personal judgment has entered the teacher's soul. She will learn to be sure that she cannot be sure, and accordingly her approach to the instructional task will become less rigid, more. tentative and . . . more responsive to the individual learning needs of the pupils with whom she is confronted.

Because so many teachers know so little about testing, however, the sense of uncertainty rarely enters the calculation of individual student worth. And the lives and careers of many Americans are shaped by their success or failure in test-taking in school.

But tests are not confined to schools. Every year, the range of formal testing grows broader. In the armed forces, recruits are routinely tested for placement; in the professions, the right to practice what one has spent years learning depends on the results of a test that lasts for several hours or several days. Applicants for civil service and for an increasing number of jobs in business and industry, candidates for promotion in a wide variety of occupations, craftsmen seeking licenses to practice their trades, and citizens who want to drive their automobiles all face qualifying paper-and-pencil tests—many of them only remotely related to the skills they purport to measure. (A number of studies support the criticism that there is little correlation between school grades—most of them based on test-taking abilities—and success on the job as rated by supervisors. Even in medical school, one 1963 investigation for the U.S. Office of Education suggested, grades have only a slight relationship to early success in the profession as ascertained by 24 performance tasks considered important by medical authorities, and they have no relation at all to later success.)

Despite the growing concern over the value of psychological tests, Americans continue to buy and use more such tests than do the rest of the world's populations combined. A 1971 survey revealed that 60 percent of large companies and almost half of medium-sized companies in the United States gave pre-employment screening tests. There are aptitude tests to predict success at work, as well as achievement tests to measure performance capabilities. There are tests designed to measure responsibility, temperament, attitudes toward authority, work habits, and honesty. And there are "general ability" tests to measure something that nobody has yet been able to define to the satisfaction of all psychologists. Dr. Oscar Buros, editor of the most prestigious reference lists of tests published in this country, calls personality "the area in which we know least about testing." In the introduction to *Personality Tests and Reviews,* he writes:

> *In this era of remarkable progress in science and technology, it is sobering to think that our most widely used instruments for personality assessment were published 20, 30, 40 and even more years ago. Despite the tremendous amount of research devoted to these old, widely used tests, they have not been replaced by instruments more acceptable to the profession. . . . The vast literature on personality testing has failed to produce a body of knowledge generally acceptable to psychologists. . . . It seems incredible, for example, that the MMPI [Minnesota Multiphasic Personality Inventory]—now being researched at the rate of 200 articles, books and theses per year—is still the same instrument published 27 years ago.*

A number of cases involving pre-employment tests reached the Supreme Court in the early 1970's. One landmark case, *Griggs vs. The Duke Power Company,* raised the issue of racial discrimination in the use of such tests. A district court judge had found no evidence of discrimination. The tests, he pointed out, were developed by professional educators. He did not question the relationship between the information asked (What is the difference between *adopt* and *adapt?* What does *B.C.* stand for?) and the unskilled work involved because, he noted, the same tests had been given to blacks and whites. By a vote of 8 to 0, the Supreme Court ruled that, "If an employment practice which operates to [keep blacks out of jobs] cannot be shown to be related to job performance, the practice is forbidden." The decision seemed to suggest that tests must either become better (more "job-related") or be abolished. But things aren't that simple.

One problem is that improving pre-employment tests and hiring the most qualified individuals for some jobs would certainly make the tests *more* discriminatory—certainly for jobs that require the kinds of education and experience that many minority group members have not been able to get. And such discrimination, measured by the proportions of blacks and other minority group members hired, could result in government action or in lawsuits under civil rights legislation and regulations.

So why not drop such tests altogether? A survey by Prentice-Hall in the early 1970's found that many employers *were* backing off from the use of such tests. Some were tempted to go back to the "numbers" game—just hiring an acceptable quota of minority workers, qualified or not, to keep the government off their backs. But Robert Guion, the author of a classic textbook on personnel selection, pointed out what some company officers had already figured out for themselves: that quota hiring will backfire when some of the possibly incompetent workers hired just to satisfy a quota later sue when they are passed over for promotion. Guion argues that *good* job-related tests do not have to discriminate against blacks.

Because of government and economic pressures, pre-employment tests are likely to improve in the future much faster than most other kinds of tests. But most of those on the market now—mass-produced and huckstered like soap—still aren't very good. They measure the *ability to take tests* far better than they measure the ability to do well on the job. Still, if you are relatively young and relatively new to the job market, there is likely to be a pre-employment test in your future.

Despite the importance of tests on their lives, most Americans have never really learned some of the basic rules of the test-taking game, largely because of their faith in the myth that most tests measure what they claim to measure. Test-taking, like the ability to play tennis or chess, is largely an acquired skill. Contrary to popular opinion, someone who knows a good deal about a subject will not automatically perform well on a test in that subject. Most tests are based on the assumption that understanding and knowledge (simply knowing things) are synonymous—and most tests don't measure either one very well. Not only the millions of teacher-made tests given each year, but many (if not most) highly regarded standardized tests used in this country are badly conceived, poorly designed, carelessly administered, and—most commonly—thoughtlessly interpreted and used for questionable purposes. Arthur S. Laughland, principal of Hyde School in Newton, Massachusetts, wrote in *The National Elementary Principal* that the standardized test "cries out for a kind of gamesmanship, and perhaps that is what it tests best." But if test-taking is a game, it is a game for which many Americans haven't learned the rules, at least not enough to be winners.

For one thing, even passing tests doesn't mean winning. The ground rules *demand* that most test-takers pass their tests. (Teachers are aware, for example, that if they consistently fail too many of their students, they raise serious questions about their own teaching competence.) But only those who do better than the "norms" or average win the acceptances to the better colleges, the prize jobs, the job promotions. Most of us have learned some of the basics of the test game—at least enough to pass, given the odds in favor of passing. The "better" students have often learned to play it extremely well. Like most Americans, *Peanuts'* little hero, Linus, knows that there are some tricks in test-taking, although he isn't quite sure what they are. Some years ago he took a true-false test. "Let's see now," he mused, "in a true-false test, the first question is almost always true. That means the next one will be false to sort of balance the true one. The next one will also be false, to break the pattern. . . ." In the final frame, a grinning Linus announced, "If you're smart, you can pass a true or false test without being smart."

How does one go about developing and sharpening test-taking skills? First of all is practice. The mere experience of having taken a test before, even without reviewing it afterward, can help test-takers raise their scores on tests with which they had been unfamiliar. By and large, the major value of coaching courses for civil service, professional, and trade examinations rests on the fact that candidates are exposed to the kind of tests they will be taking.

But if an individual is testwise in addition—that is, if he or she has learned some of the specific skills of test-taking—that individual can expect to score considerably higher in tests than can those with equal ability in the subject area who haven't learned these test-taking skills. Certainly with most classroom tests and with large numbers of the standardized tests, it is possible for someone to do well without understanding much about the subject. (Unfortunately, this possibility works both ways. There are intelligent and educated persons who suffer because they have never really mastered some of the elements of defensive test-taking.)

Some authorities find the whole idea of formal paper-and-pencil testing unnatural and repulsive. Professor S. L. Washburn of the University of California at Berkeley, former president of the American Anthropological Association, thinks that formal testing is a repudiation of the human biological heritage. School discipline, he writes, "is no substitute for . . . internal motivation, and examinations are no substitute fore life. . . . Human beings are not pigeons who may be taught to peck out the solutions to futile problems." And Jerrold R. Zacharias of M.I.T. calls members of the testing industry "merchants of death . . . because of what they do to the kids. . . . Testing has distorted their ambitions, distorted their careers."

Most psychologists and educational leaders think that testing can be a useful and constructive way of measuring progress, diagnosing problems, and evaluating learning. But many test experts also agree that tests and test programs are often misused: many if not most tests used in schools and industry are inappropriate to the professed objectives of the school or the business, and tests are being used far more frequently to sort out, screen, measure, classify, and assign people than to teach them or to help them.

Critics blame the testing industry for making outrageous claims for tests and for convincing buyers that tests will provide accurate measures for all human mental activities. Industry spokesmen, on the other hand, blame unsophisticated test buyers and test users for expecting more from tests than any test can deliver. Arthur E. Smith, Director of Educational Services of the National Merit Scholarship Corporation, has argued that "The future of educational measurement is not in the control of the test authors or publishers. It is in the hands of test users— guidance directors, administrators, counselors, teachers and psychologists. It depends on the ability and skill of the user in narrowing the gap between what can be learned from tests and how test results are used."

It is true that booklets published by such organizations as ETS and consultants sent out to advise and lecture warn buyers to use test results with caution. This warning is often brushed aside by readers and listeners as scholarly restraint and institutional modesty. Probably there is enough blame to spread around. Buros wrote in the introduction to *Tests In Print*:

At present, no matter how poor a test may be, if it is nicely packaged and if it promises to do all sorts of things which no test can do, the test will find many gullible buyers.

. . . Counselors, personnel directors, psychologists and school administrators seem to have an unshakable will to believe the exaggerated claims of test authors and publishers. If these test users were better informed regarding the merits and limitations of their testing instruments, they would probably be less happy and successful in their work. The test user [this means the school counselor or psychologist or personnel officer who ordered the test, not the test taker] who has faith—however unjustified—can speak with confidence in interpreting test results and in making recommendations. The well-informed test user cannot do this; he knows that the best of our tests are still highly fallible instruments which are extremely difficult to interpret with assurance in individual cases. Consequently, he must interpret test results cautiously and with so many reservations that others wonder whether he really knows what he is talking about.

For the test-taker, of course, it really doesn't matter who is responsible for the generally bad use of tests and test results. Increasing numbers of Americans are being marched off to school desks, reception rooms, auditoriums, army reception centers, hired halls, and tables in personnel offices to be folded, mutilated, and spindled by the testing process. As testing becomes a major national preoccupation, learning to cope with tests becomes a necessary social and economic skill.

2.
You *Can* Raise Your IQ

WHAT IS INTELLIGENCE?

When we talk of someone as being *intelligent,* most of us think we understand each other. The experts in intelligence testing aren't as sure that *they* do. In fact, the experts can't even agree that there is something called intelligence that is different from what one learns. While Harvard psychologist R. J. Herrnstein claims that "the measure of intelligence is psychology's most telling accomplishment to date," David McClelland wonders why IQ testing has been accepted with such faith instead of being subjected to "the fierce skepticism that greets, for example, the latest attempt to show that ESP exists." But even if you accept the notion that intelligence exists, you still have to face some vexing questions about the relative influence of nature versus nurture. Is intelligence an attribute with which you're born, like the color of your eyes? Or is it an ability or skill that can be learned, like chess or tennis or piano playing? If it's a combination of the two, as most psychologists today agree, what is the influence of each? About the only generally accepted definition of intelligence is this tautology: intelligence is what intelligence tests measure! And many psychologists won't accept even *that* definition.

The thinking behind this nondefinition goes something like this: We can't measure intelligence directly, the way we measure height. We can only infer it from watching the way different individuals perform "standard tasks," and then rank the individuals in terms of their scores. So we can't tell just *how* intelligent you are, but only how you compare with others. But since the comparison is based on *achievement,* we can never be sure whether we're ranking intelligence or learning. Says T. Anne Cleary, a vice-president of the College Entrance Examination Board, "All tests are achievement tests. Anyone who thinks he can test strictly innate ability is incorrect, illogical and—if you'll pardon my saying so—doesn't have a very high IQ."

To complicate the issue even more, the kinds of "standard tasks" assigned depend on the test-makers' personal views of what intelligence is—and thus we have a debate over another series of questions. Those test-makers who think that intelligence is a *single,* general ability will design tests that ask you to deal with standard problems in a wide variety of areas and will rank you in terms of one overall score. Test designers who believe there are different kinds of intelligence will ask you to take a battery of tests, each one related to a special ability such as memory, spatial relationship, computational skills, language abilities, and creativity, and will rank you separately in each area. The may, or may not, average out the scores to give you one overall score.

A growing number of psychologists believe that intelligence is the ease with which an individual learns a totally new skill; they are concerned that there is no standard intelligence test in general use to measure this ability.

But, meanwhile, because all IQ tests are basically achievement tests that measure what you have *learned* (whether or not they measure anything else), they are all remarkably similar to the "aptitude" tests that will get you into—or keep you out of—college or graduate or professional schools. Studies show that scores on standard IQ tests correlate highly with scores on the academic aptitude tests such as the Scholastic Aptitude Test (SAT), the Graduate Record Exam (GRE) and the Law School Admission Test (LSAT). Some of the items in the adult Stanford-Binet IQ test are almost identical with items in the SAT, especially in the verbal section. Anne Anastasi, in her well-known book, *Psychological Testing,* deals with the SAT in a chapter entitled, "Group Tests of General Intelligence." So raising your IQ means raising your achievement test scores.

WHAT'S YOUR IQ?

Your IQ is not the same as your intelligence—unless you accept the old psychologists' nondefinition above. An IQ is no more and no less than a score on a test. The notion of intelligence testing itself is a fairly recent one in human history.

Formal intelligence testing really began with French psychologist Alfred Binet in 1905. The French Minister of Education asked Binet and his associate, Theodore Simon, to develop a test that would identify schoolchildren who needed remediation. The test they developed was revised and expanded several times, and in 1916 Lewis Terman of Stanford University adapted and revised it for use with

American adults. A modern version of this Stanford-Binet test is still in wide use, although the fact that it is individually administered makes it unsuitable for mass testing.

When the United States entered World War I, several psychologists were asked to develop a group intelligence test to screen and assign draftees. Two tests were developed for group use: the Army Alpha, to be used with those who could read, and the Army Beta, for illiterates.

During the 1920's the use of IQ tests expanded into schools, industry, and government, where they were used with great enthusiasm—and little intelligence. Terman himself, on the basis of the army testing experience during the war, announced that the average "mental age" of Americans was 14. And much of the interest in mental testing was based on the hopes that it would support commonly held convictions about blacks and foreigners. On the basis of administering the Binet test to new immigrants arriving in Ellis Island in 1912, psychologist Henry Goddard concluded that 83% of the Jews, 80% of the Hungarians, 79% of the Italians, and 87% of the Russians were "feebleminded." Moreover, concluded Terman, "all feebleminded are at least potential criminals." Princeton psychology professor Carl Brigham, later to become the father of the SAT, warned that continued immigration would result in a new American who "will be less intelligent than the present native-born American." Such thinking, based on the "scientific" evidence of the IQ tests, contributed to the national quota system, discriminating against immigrants from eastern and southern Europe, that underlay our immigration policy for almost 50 years. Apparently, the psychologists of the 1920's resolutely refused to acknowledge that a written IQ test is largely a test of reading ability in English, and that even a nonverbal IQ test administered by someone who speaks only English probably tests language more than it does intelligence. Although there have been refinements and improvements in intelligence testing since Terman's day, this is true today of most group tests.

Back in the 1920's, just as today, there were critics who argued that the IQ tests were culturally biased and invalid. To Terman's charge that he had an "emotional complex," writer Walter Lippmann responded: "Well, I have. I admit it. I hate the impudence of a claim that in 50 minutes you can judge and classify a human being's predestined fitness in life. I hate the pretentiousness of that claim. I hate the abuse of the scientific method which it involves. I hate the sense of superiority which it creates and the sense of inferiority which it imposes."

Some black psychologists today argue that most IQ tests are biased and are used to label black and other minority children as unintelligent when, in fact, the children have simply not been exposed to many of the concepts that are presented—such as chimney or cow or saddle—or have not been taught specific information or vocabulary. Black sociologist Adrian Dove designed his own "chitling test" as a "half-serious idea to show that we're just not talking the same language." And black psychologist Robert Williams designed a similarly biased (toward blacks) tests that he calls the Black Intelligence Test of Cultural Homogeneity (the Bitch Test). Try some samples of an IQ test biased against whites:

11

If a man is called a "blood," he is a   (a) fighter   (b) Mexican-American
(c) Negro   (d) hungry hemophile   (e) Redman or Indian

A "Gas Head" is a person who has a   (a) fast-moving car   (b) stable of lace
(c) process   (d) habit of stealing cars   (e) long jail record for arson

Virginia is passing. Her black cousin Blue just crashed her party on her well-lit lawn at
85th and Merrill. Her boss, husband, and friends are all there. Blue is loud. What
will she do?   (a) deny Blue   (b) slip him $20   (c) give him an apron
(d) yell "rape"

Cheap chitlins (not the kind you purchase at a frozen food counter) will taste rubbery
unless they are cooked long enough. How soon can you quit cooking them to eat and
enjoy them.?   (a) 45 minutes   (b) 2 hours   (c) 24 hours   (d) 1 week (on
a low flame)   (e) 1 hour

A "hype" is a person who   (a) always says he feels sickly   (b) has water on
the brain   (c) uses heroin   (d) is always ripping and running
(e) is always sick

You've just been exposed to a reverse type of culture bias, courtesy of the Dove Counterbalance General Intelligence Test, also known as the Chitling Test or the Ghetto Soul Test. How many did you get correct? The answer to each of these was (c).

There are three basic assumptions underlying the measurement of IQ.
- We can measure people's intelligence, without even being able to define it, by observing their behavior.
- This measurement has meaning only if we compare an individual's success in performing a "standard task" against a norm or average. So everybody to be compared has to perform the same tasks and do the same things. (Because standard tasks vary, your IQ may be different on different tests.)
- As individuals grow older, they can perform more and more difficult tasks.

How does the system work in identifying your IQ? If a 10-year-old boy can achieve a score that is usually achieved by 12-year-olds, he is said to have a mental age of 12. The formula that has been developed since Binet's time (he opposed the idea, just as he denied that intelligence is inborn) was that of IQ, or *intelligence quotient.*

$$IQ = \frac{\text{mental age}}{\text{chronological age}} \times 100 \text{ (to eliminate fractions or decimals)}$$

For our 10-year-old with the "mentality" of a 12-year-old, this means:
$\frac{12}{10} = 1.20 \times 100 = 120$.

A score of 100 is considered average or "normal." Because of the possibility of "testing error," scores between 90 and 109 are called normal. Terman classified individuals from "genius" to "idiot," but nowadays, the terms are somewhat more restrained. One commonly used distribution is:

140+	very superior
120–139	superior
110–119	high average
90–109	normal
80–89	low average
70–79	borderline
69 and below	feebleminded

These classifications aren't universal. A 1972 California study showed that among children labeled "mentally retarded" by schools, fully 46% had IQ's above 70. (And of all the agencies that deal with mental health or mental ability, only schools relied almost exclusively on these tests, without any medical diagnosis to support the label of mental retardation.) The study supported the charge of cultural bias by concluding that minority group children are most likely to be labeled mentally retarded, "not because they are unable to cope with the world, but because they have not had the opportunity to learn the cognitive skills necessary to pass Anglo-oriented intelligence tests." (Since 1975, federal law makes it illegal for schools to use one IQ test as the only basis for placement, and calls for teacher judgment as well. Since teacher judgment is profoundly influenced by test scores, the situation hasn't changed as much as some think it has.)

Of course, the idea of mental age is built on some shifty assumptions. One is that intelligence can be measured on a simple linear scale like weight, height, or length of fingernails. The weight of individuals can be compared directly: a 150-pound 15-year-old and a 150-pound adult of 25 weigh the same. But a 15-year-old with a "mental age" of 18 has an IQ of 120, while a 25-year-old man with a "mental age" of 18 has an IQ of 72. And even though they have the same mental age, we know that they don't think the same at all, and *neither* one thinks like the average 18-year-old.

To be fair, not all psychologists agree that the idea of mental age should be carried into adulthood. Some think mental growth stops at age 16; others place it at 18 or 20. In an attempt to compensate for the illogic of the old formula, many of the old-line test-makers have begun to do some amazing things with numbers. But an increasing number of psychometricians now think that the terms "IQ" and "mental age" are meaningless, and instead prefer to talk of *academic readiness,* or *scholastic aptitude,* or *ability to succeed* (in *school,* because a clear relationship between IQ and success in later life has never been established). The term IQ will probably disappear in time, although it will continue to do a good deal of harm for years to come.

DO IQ TESTS PREDICT SCHOOL PERFORMANCE?

Whatever it is they measure, IQ tests in general are reasonably successful in predicting school achievement. The correlation between IQ scores and school grades seems to hover around .5. (1.0 means a perfect correlation; 0 means no correlation at all. So .5 means a substantial, but not an overwhelming correlation.) The correlations are much higher with students in the higher grades, probably because the work demanded from students in higher grades becomes more and more like the skills and abilities measured by IQ tests. There is evidence that for 7- or 8-year-olds the tests are pretty good predictors of school success. The child who scores better than 75% of his classmates at age 8 will most likely score better than 75% of his classmates at age 15.

But critics don't agree that this correlation has much to do with intelligence. Some claim the tests are deliberately designed to measure only what children have already learned in school or at home, and what the schools value, such things as reading and conformity. The tests don't measure many attributes that are highly prized outside of school, such as creativity, initiative, independence, empathy, perseverance, and courage. And, says critic David McClelland, a high IQ may lead to school success (and frequently to career success) simply because it is a "credential" that opens doors to better schooling. So the scores often become self-fulfilling prophecies: Children with low IQ scores are put in low-expectation classes where they will perform as little as is expected of them. And children with high scores are put in "fast" classes, where most of them will perform as expected.

Even more important, the tests are tools of "guidance." In secondary schools IQ scores weigh heavily in determining the programs into which students are placed and the kind of work into which they are directed. Black psychologist Robert L. Williams (who himself had been advised to go into manual trades on the basis of a low IQ score) calls the use of such tests "the silent mugging of the black community."

Why are the tests used so widely? Lawrence Plotkin, a psychologist and educational researcher at New York's City College, thinks that tests help schools cop out of their decisions. He told a magazine reporter: "It takes a real clinical expert to diagnose some of these problems. But why hire a lot of psychologists when you can do it for 19 cents a test? And it takes the onus off the school officials because they didn't make the decision." An increasing number of educators are coming to agree. Group IQ tests have been banned from the public school systems of New York and Washington, D.C., on the ground that too many children have been mislabeled as slow or retarded on the basis of the tests alone. A study in Washington showed that of the students placed in special education classes on the basis of test scores, two-thirds didn't belong there.

Even though tests are pretty good at predicting achievement for large groups, they aren't quite as good in predicting what a given *individual* will do. And to explain away the tests' frequent failure to predict accurately, two pretty silly terms have been invented: *underachiever* and *overachiever*. These terms suggest that

14

there is something rather extraordinary if an individual's achievement doesn't match his or her test score. ETS, a major producer of standardized tests, talks about underachievement in terms of "poor study habits, lack of motivation, or lack of challenge," and overachievement in terms of "undue tensions or pressures to 'do well.' " In other words, kid, do what the tests say you can do—no more and no less!

At about the same time that ETS was publishing these views, its own chief psychometrician, Henry Dyer, wrote in *The Teachers College Record*:

> The notion of the underachiever—the child who is not working up to ability—has taken deep roots in spite of the efforts of some psychometricians to kill it. We thought we had it buried in the 1930's, but in the past few years it has again raised its ugly head. The customary, and ordinarily fallacious, diagnosis is that the student with a high ability score and low marks in school is ipso facto *unmotivated or lazy or suffering from some emotional disturbances traceable perhaps to faulty toilet training. Granted that these are possibilities, nevertheless it is a vast mistake to assume that they can be inferred solely from the discrepancy between the scores and the marks. The first question to ask is, Why has Johnny learned how to answer the test questions better than the teacher's questions? Perhaps the trouble is not in Johnny at all but in the kinds of questions on the test, or in the kinds of questions the teacher asks, or even in the teacher's skill as a teacher.*

Dyer was irked by some of the concepts behind the use of these tests. In 1971 Dyer told a group of 500 educators attending an ETS conference that IQ scores and grade equivalency scores (which tell you whether you're performing at your "grade level" of expectation) were monstrosities that were "probably the most convenient devices ever invented to lead people into misinterpretation of students' test results." Similar complaints have been voiced by other top test-makers, including ETS president William Turnbull and Roger Lennon, senior vice-president of Harcourt Brace Jovanovich (publisher of two of the most widely used achievement test batteries). These experts claim that the IQ test is nothing but an achievement test with pretensions that it measures more than it does. By claiming to measure innate abilities, some critics contend, schools can relieve themselves of the challenge of teaching students with learning problems.

On the other hand, Robert Ebel, one-time vice-president of ETS and a specialist in educational measurement, doesn't think it matters what you call the test, as long as it does the job of predicting school success. "Since we cannot measure latent-trait IQ [what you were born with] directly, and since our indirect measurements are distorted by uncontrolled influences," he wrote in 1975, "it seems clear that we are unlikely to get highly reliable or highly valid measures of the IQ. It also seems clear that such measures are not really necessary. All learning builds on prior learning."

In other words, quite a few of the top experts on testing think that IQ tests really measure what you've *learned.* And whether or not IQ's really measure intelligence, nobody worries about the overachiever—the student who does *better* than the tests predict. Also, the students who fall within the range of the "expectancy tables" and the "grade equivalency" norms are doing all that is expected of them (even if they can do much more) so nobody worries about them either, or pushes them to do more. The fortunate students are those who, in Dyer's words, have learned to answer the test questions better than the teacher's questions, because *everybody* worries about the underachiever who hasn't lived up to his good test scores. They expect more from him, and he usually ends up doing better as a result.

So scores do predict school success—although not always in the way you'd think.

As an aside, if you live in the Southeast and if your high school teacher is over 40, he or she puts a good deal of faith in the IQ tests' predictive ability and will probably check your IQ scores before you even set foot in the classroom. The teachers who are most skeptical are those in the Northeast and those under 40.

HOW IMPORTANT IS MEMORY IN INTELLIGENCE?

Not very, according to the experts. First of all, there are several types of memory: *long-term, short-term, symbolic, figural, lists,* and so on. There is *recall* (pulling information out of your memory bank at will) and there is *recognition* (identifying data that are presented to you) and there is *associative memory* (which helps you retrieve a piece of information when you are given a cue word or symbol or smell with which you associate it). Studies have shown that there is only a moderate connection between your ability to memorize on one level and to memorize on another. Interestingly enough, as people grow old, they seem to lose some of their memory ability, usually recall, but not the associative memory. In any event, studies by Dr. John W. French and others at ETS have shown little correlation between memory span (the ability tested when you are asked to repeat lists of numbers forward or backward) and any other form of memory or of learning.

It seems that you must have a minimum memory ability to do reasonable schoolwork, but most people who are not feebleminded or sick have this minimum ability. The studies also indicate that a phenomenal memory doesn't seem of much help in most usual IQ test items, although it probably would help you to do better in the vocabulary items. In other words, if you're a low scorer, chances are that a poor memory isn't your basic problem.

HOW IMPORTANT IS READING SKILL?

Reading is probably the most important single skill that is tested on most paper-and-pencil group intelligence tests. If you can't read well, you'll have trouble with both the directions and the test items themselves. Many of the special "IQ training programs" for very young children are really reading readiness programs.

Reading consists of two major parts: *decoding,* or translating the written symbols into the appropriate sounds; and *comprehending,* or understanding the meaning of what you have decoded.

Recent years have seen a good deal of debate over the most effective methods for teaching decoding skills (also known as word analysis skills, word attack skills, and word recognition skills). Actually, most decoding problems stem from the fact that written English is not truly phonetic. In the early 1800's Sequoya, the famous Cherokee, invented a Cherokee "syllabary" so completely phonetic that anyone who learned the symbols and the sounds could read immediately; some Indians were taught to read within 24 hours. In contrast, English letters and letter combinations can be sounded out in a bewildering variety of ways: Consider the *gh* in *through, ghastly,* and *laugh*; or the *c* in *cat, adjacent,* and *coincide* (the last has two different sounds for c); or the *a* in *father, brave, bare,* and *action.*

Because this very outdated and complicated system that developed over the years has borrowed from many other languages, many children have trouble with just the mechanical skill of decoding the language combinations. Given the present system of "phonic-linguistic" teaching, most children eventually do learn to decode, although low IQ children take longer to learn. (Which came first? Are these children low IQ because they have trouble reading, or do they have trouble reading because they're low IQ?)

It's the second area of reading—understanding the meaning of words in context—that's troublesome in the area of intelligence testing. This "meaning" is so closely connected with the idea of intelligence as measured on the tests, that in mass tests we can't really be sure whether we're measuring intelligence or reading. This aspect of reading can be distorted by all sorts of reader problems: anxiety, self-consciousness, distracting noises, physical disturbances all interfere with comprehension. Low IQ scorers frequently haven't gone past the decoding stage to the comprehension stage of reading. (In a later chapter there will be some practical guides on dealing with reading comprehension questions.)

There are many clues to poor comprehension reading. Poor readers often read too quickly; frequently, they'll finish passages long before the better readers have absorbed them. In the process, the poor reader will miss important connecting words and expressions, or even punctuation that may change the meaning of a passage. Poor readers often fail to divorce themselves from the materials; instead of reading the passages as presented, and thus absorbing the author's meaning, they read into it their own opinions and views. Poor readers often jump to conclusions on the basis of a handful of words and ideas (this, by the way, is a problem that was found by *every investigator who looked into the problem of low scoring on tests*). Poor readers often fail to go back over previously read materials, preferring to rely on hunch and on the common rationale that "first impressions are probably accurate." Needless to say, studies don't support this notion.

Good readers, in contrast, are continually restructuring the new materials to fit them into meaningful patterns, *without* changing the meaning. As good readers come across words or phrases that change the meaning or focus of what has been read, they go back and mentally retranslate the entire passage. They don't leave gaps in their understanding of a passage. (There's a paradox here; good test-takers often deliberately skim passages when it's obvious that test questions call for recognition skills only. More on this in Chapter 4 on general strategies in test-taking.)

Will speed reading courses help you to read faster, better, more accurately? Not according to the bulk of the evidence. Speed reading helps you to read *faster,* not *better.* In fact, says Dr. George D. Spache, former head of the University of Florida Reading Laboratory and Clinic, most speed reading "teaches one to skip. The less you see, the less you comprehend." Tests with eye movement films show that 900 words a minute is about as fast as anyone can read with reasonable (75%) comprehension. A reasonable rate for most college students reading school material is about 300 words a minute, and a study showed that University of Michigan professors read at about the same rate when they're reading for understanding. Most speed reading teachers consider 300 words a minute painfully slow and evidence of reading deficiency. But Ira A. Aaron, professor of reading education at the University of Georgia, says, "You can't read faster than you think. . . . Rapid reading seminars are not for poor readers." Most tests of reading "comprehension" given in speed reading courses are tests of recognition or familiarity, the easiest of the four tests of comprehension.

Because reading comprehension skills and general intelligence scores are so closely related, a number of the IQ-raising programs focus on the reading problem. Out of carefully conducted studies a number of conclusions have come that contradict some popular educational advice on reading. Based on these conclusions, here are some hints:

• Reading aloud can help, especially if you have a listener. Don't read for diction, or style, or feeling. Just read for comprehension. The idea is that by reading aloud, you bring into the open what is usually an undercover operation. A monitor listening to you can pinpoint where your thinking has gone off or where you've drawn an incorrect inference.

Does reading aloud interfere with your comprehension? Reading teachers normally try to get students *away* from vocalizing. Studies show that practically all readers make lip and tongue movements (especially with difficult materials), or they may *subvocalize,* that is, pronounce words and phrases to themselves mentally. Poor readers vocalize more, and traditionally it has been assumed that such vocalizing interferes with their comprehension. The recent findings suggest that poor readers vocalize more *because* they find more materials difficult. When you read an especially difficult passage, even if you're a good reader, you may find yourself going back and actually whispering the words to yourself; subvocalization or even reading aloud to yourself may help you to hear as well as read the ideas.

Does reading aloud slow you down? Not really. John Carroll of ETS found that for most people the top speed for meaningful reading is about 425 words a minute, and practically everybody can talk a good deal faster than that. So stop worrying about reading speed unless you have trouble understanding what you read. In this case, learning to understand better should help you with the problem of speed.

• After each passage or combination of ideas, stop to *translate,* putting the passage into your own words, and to *interpret,* connecting the ideas with ideas you read earlier. Again, this should be done aloud, so that your monitor can spot mistakes before you've gone too far. If you have trouble with translation, you might want to try writing out difficult passages. By concentrating on meaning as you write, you're adding another activity as an aid to comprehension.

• Leave no gaps in your understanding. This doesn't mean that you must understand each word or sentence as you read it; often an idea is made clear in the following sentences. (In a later chapter, we'll deal with the use of contextual clues as a test-taking device.) But if you don't really grasp an idea before the passage moves on, go back. Vocalize, if you have to. Write a summary if it helps. A 1975 study at Arizona State University showed that students who took notes on a textbook passage performed better on tests than those who merely read or even underlined it. The investigators suggested that "quite possibly, the high performance of the note-taking learner is measurably due to the fact that he spends more time with the material." Others think that writing the ideas helps the reader to "process" them in another way.

CAN INTELLIGENCE BE RAISED THROUGH TRAINING?

Both sides in the nature-versus-nurture argument have submitted impressive arrays of statistics. Arthur Jensen of the University of California contends that 80% of the difference in intelligence is inherited and only 20% due to environment—a claim that led writer Martin Mayer to remark wryly in his book, *The Schools,* that "an outsider is continually amazed by the fine tolerance at which psychologists measure things they cannot even define." On the other hand, Christopher Jencks of Harvard, who has compiled what is probably the most complete statistical study yet made on the subject, contends that intelligence seems heavily influenced by environmental factors. Jerome Kagan, also of Harvard, writes simply that "existing scientific data do not permit strong statements about the degree of genetic or environmental control of intelligence."

In other words, we just don't know how much of your intelligence is inherited and how much is learned. Too bad, because what we *think* we know has a profound influence on what happens in school. If people are born different, then it is useless and cruel to demand that "slow" children be pushed beyond their capacities, because such pressure can only guarantee failure and frustration. If, on the other hand, most intelligence is learned, then we have shortchanged large numbers of children just because they were born into the wrong families or neighborhoods or racial or ethnic groups, or because they had the wrong experiences when they were young.

But for your purposes *now,* the question of nature versus nurture really doesn't mean much. Whatever intelligence traits you may have been born with, the important question is whether you can *raise* your intelligence through training.

Evidence is coming in that intelligence can be affected dramatically by planned activity, and more so than can be accounted for by chance or "testing error." Changes of from 1 to 10 IQ points occur in an estimated 70% of school-children during their school years. But a number of planned and purposeful programs have succeeded in raising IQ's an *average* of 15 points over a long range. Check the IQ classification given earlier to see what this might mean in a child's school placement.

At first glance, the evidence is mixed. Some programs have achieved long-lasting increases in children's IQ; others haven't. But looking carefully, we can see some major differences between the ones that work and the ones that don't.

Professor John T. Seyfarth of Virginia Commonwealth University says, "IQ [seems] relatively unaffected by the environmental influences that are typical of most educational programs." The schools, by and large, haven't had spectacular success with compensatory programs such as the massive federally funded Head Start, a program designed to send culturally deprived children to "stimulating" nursery schools with lots of toys, games, and activities. In those situations that have been analyzed, it was found that for a year or two children made some gains—about 5 to 10 points—but the gains rapidly disappeared within the first year of formal school. Critics like Jensen have pointed to such programs as evidence that the limits of intelligence are genetically determined.

But investigators were intrigued by evidence that under certain circumstances, long-lasting changes *can* occur. In Israel, for example, the children of Oriental Jews grow up in culturally deprived areas and have an average IQ score of 85, while children of middle-class European Jews have average scores of 105. But in the kibbutzim, where the children of Oriental and European Jews grow up together, the average IQ of all the children is 115.

So a number of investigators—including Benjamin Bloom of the University of Chicago, Carl Bereiter and Siegfried Englemann of the University of Illinois, and Rick Heber of Milwaukee—conducted a series of studies. Their basic conclusions matched: *random* "stimulation" has little effect on IQ scores because low scorers and high scorers *think* differently. Low scorers, they found, tend to engage in one-shot thinking—they guess, jump to conclusions, and find it difficult to engage in systematic and deliberate analysis. Bereiter and Englemann found, in fact, that such children believe answers should be given *immediately,* and so they guess. Low achievers assume that you either "know" or "don't know" an answer; they don't try to *derive* answers by organizing information into coherent patterns.

In his book *How Children Fail,* John Holt illustrates the differences in thinking patterns between low and high achievers. In playing *"Twenty Questions,"* a game in which the goal is to guess an object, the high achievers (the systematic thinkers) ask questions designed to narrow the possibilities. The poorer thinkers take wild, blind stabs, throwing away their opportunities on one-shot, random questions. Because low achievers see no value in systematic thinking, they put their faith in luck rather than strategy. They have learned to expect failure—and are rarely disappointed.

Out of these findings grew experimental programs designed to teach sequential, organized thinking. While the programs varied, all had common elements. They called for total and constant involvement by the learner, either on

20

an individual basis or in groups (Bereiter and Engelmann called for all the children to respond to each question in unison) to provide feedback to the teacher so that errors could be pinpointed immediately, and to break the low achiever habit of passivity (waiting for the challenge or problem to disappear).

All the programs were sustained, regular, and continuing—whether the sessions were held every day or several days a week; whether they lasted several hours or, as at the Albert Einstein College of Medicine, for as little as 15 to 20 minutes a day. Children who attended the Albert Einstein College program five days a week showed IQ score increases averaging 14½ points. Those attending three days a week showed increases of 7 points; and those in a control group that met regularly with the same teacher but were merely "exposed" to "stimulating" materials showed increases of only 2 points.

These last findings are of interest when it is noted that most coaching schools, and virtually all coaching courses in schools, limit their programs to exposure to the types of questions that will be on the tests, to "enrichment" materials, or even to "techniques." These may be helpful, but as the studies demonstrate, they have limited effectiveness in changing basic thinking patterns. Their approaches can be compared to trying to learn to play a piano or serve a tennis ball by just reading. You may gain some familiarity with the techniques involved, but without a monitor, you're also likely to keep on repeating errors without even knowing it. Programs in testing and study skills offered in many universities ("Preparation for the GRE," for example) simply go over questions, telling you if you got the right answer and why it's the right answer. Few of them deal with *why you got the wrong answer.* They focus on *teaching,* not on *learning;* on *telling,* not on *listening.* Remember the old gag: "I taught my dog to whistle." "Funny, I never heard him whistle." "I said I taught him; I didn't say he learned it."

Every successful program, whether with preschoolers or with college students, has involved the element of *monitored feedback.* We'll examine one such program in some detail and focus on the simple elements.

HOW CAN YOU RAISE YOUR IQ?

Apparently the same basic techniques that have proved helpful in raising achievement and aptitude test scores are useful in raising basic IQ scores. (After all, they're *all* achievement tests!) Building on earlier studies, psychometrician Arthur Whimbey developed a task analysis approach to problem solving that he calls "cognitive therapy."

To find why people test poorly, Whimbey asked them to think aloud as they solved typical problems. This technique was used by Alfred Binet and by such developmental psychologists as Jean Piaget. Whimbey's findings paralleled those of Bereiter and Engelmann, of Benjamin Bloom, and of others. Among other characteristics in common, poor testers:
- rush through directions and sometimes skip them altogether;
- resort to one-shot thinking;

21

- put little faith in reasoning as a way of solving problems;
- "know" or "don't know" an answer; if they don't perceive an answer immediately, they feel lost;
- operate on feelings and hunches;
- rarely go back to reread or clarify.

Two examples from Whimbey's work with students illustrate low-level (poor tester) thinking. The following problem requires nothing more than a careful following of instructions, but it is missed by many low achievers:

> *Cross out the letter after the letter in the word "seldom" which is in the same position in the word as it is in the alphabet.*

Low scorers, Whimbey found, often cross out the *d* in "*seldom*"; some cross out the *d* in "*word.*" In either case, the students have failed to break the problem down into small manageable units and proceed systematically, as follows:

> "*Cross out the letter* [I have to find a letter to cross out]
> "*after the letter* [but first I have to find another letter]
> "*in the word* [I have to find the word first]
> "*seldom* [that's the word]
> "*which is in the same position in the word* [that's *seldom*]

"*as it is in the alphabet.*" [*d* is the fourth letter in the alphabet, and it's the fourth letter in *seldom*. But wait—just what do the instructions call for? Cross out the letter *after*. . . . That means I don't cross out *d*; I cross out *o*.]

Following instructions, especially if they're involved, requires analysis and systematic procedure—tasks that low achievers often rush through.

Another type of problem common to both IQ tests and most achievement tests is the *analogy* involving relationships. Whimbey's example:

> *Elephant* is to *small* as _____ is to _____.
> (a) large: little
> (b) turtle: slow
> (c) hippopotamus: mouse
> (d) lion: timid

Low achievers often choose (a). They fail to analyze the relationship between *elephant* and *small* and to carry the same relationship through their search of the other words. The thinking of a high scorer might be as follows: "Elephant—that's an animal. Small—that's an adjective. But small doesn't describe elephants; elephants are big. So the relationship that is wanted must be an adjective that does *not* describe the animal—in fact, maybe it's just the opposite of the description. Is there any pair that has an animal and a description of it that doesn't fit? Yes—it's (d)—a lion is not timid."

Whimbey's approach to training students built largely on the work of Benjamin Bloom and Lois Broder, who had developed a pilot program for low-achieving college students. The students had been required to think through an approach to a problem out loud. After discussing student approaches, Bloom and Broder read the ideal solution aloud, and the student himself would explain how his approach differed from the model. Eventually, they found, students learned to recognize the differences and apply the successful principles.

Whimbey worked with one student in a pilot study aimed at increasing his scores on the LSAT and the GRE. The first time the student had taken the exams, he had scored 385 on the LSAT (in the bottom 10 percent) and 750 on the combined GRE—quite low. After five months of intensive training two hours a day, four days a week, the student's GRE score had climbed to 820. That fall his grades in algebra—a major problem area—climbed to B+ and then to A. The following December, six months after the training had ended, the student again took the GRE and this time scored 890, a gain of 140 points over his original score. Apparently, the change in the type of thinking continued to help the student; he had now learned *how* to learn. While a single case does not represent compelling evidence, the results here were in line with those of the other experimenters.

One of Whimbey's secrets was to bring hidden thought processes out into the open, where they could be seen, analyzed, and corrected, like a bad tennis serve or a mistake in typing. So his main tactic was to have the student read aloud and *think* out loud as he examined relationships. Whimbey identified errors and engaged in discussion immediately with the student; he probed with questions. The methods he used, Whimbey argues, resemble the methods many middle-class parents often use with their children in conversation. Whimbey thinks that cram courses, as such, are useless, and most psychometricians agree.

If you want to develop your own training program and don't have any of the experts around, what can you do?

First of all, recognize that cramming—for a few days or even a few weeks—won't work. You'll have to give yourself plenty of time for practice, and you'll have to stick to your schedule. Remember the study at the Albert Einstein College of Medicine: regularity is probably more important than the total amount of time.

All the studies make it clear that just "learning" the techniques isn't enough. You have to practice, just as you would in learning to water-ski or play the piano, but you must also be sure that you're not simply repeating your old errors. So you need *feedback* from a critical observer. One answer is a patient instructor—a friend, spouse, parent. Even better, perhaps, is a group of others who are interested in raising their test scores. A group can help you to maintain interest day after day and week after week. It can also give you moral support, reminding you that others have the same problem.

Read the problem aloud. Think out loud as you probe for a solution. Have your instructor or your group members be alert to raise questions or pinpoint errors, either in your understanding of the problem or in your solution. Check your answers against a model, if one is available. Go back to identify where you went wrong. Go through the whole problem again correctly.

A very useful device is the drawing of diagrams; some people see problems more clearly in visual form. Let's take an example in the kind of problem usually designated as logic and reasoning.

All A is B. All C is B. Which choice follows?   (a) All C is A   (b) Some C is A
(c) No C is A   (d) Some B is A

There are many ways in which the premise can be drawn. Below are four diagrams, all of which fit the specifications in the question.

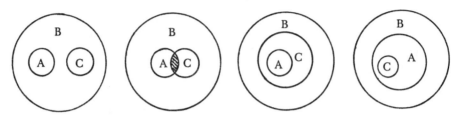

By referring to your diagrams as you consider the choices, it becomes pretty clear that the correct answer is (d).

What do you use for materials? Actually, any old tests, puzzle books, or problems. Remember, you're working on *thinking patterns,* not on specific types of questions. But you also want to familiarize yourself with the kinds of questions likely to appear on IQ tests as well as on the other scholastic aptitude tests. On the following pages are sample items of the types of questions you're likely to find. Search out similar types of questions, on old tests and on sample test booklets published by any of the major test publishers. If you're in high school, you might want to check with your guidance counselor (or with the college admissions office or your advisor if you're in college) for instruction books and sample items. Remember, the SAT and GRE are basically the same kind of test as the IQ, so you can use any of them for your purpose.

WHAT KINDS OF ITEMS APPEAR ON INTELLIGENCE TESTS?

The "standard tasks" on any intelligence test depend on the view of intelligence that is held by the test-maker. Some tests are based on the assumption that there is a "g" factor, a general ability to do well scholastically. And, like the old Army Alpha, they give you a single score—an IQ score, or a centile score that tells you that you did better than a certain percentage of the people who took the test. Single-score tests are usually used to open or shut doors. Some of the major tests in this category include the Otis tests, the Henmon-Nelson, the Kuhlmann-Anderson, and the Pintner tests.

A lot of tests used today are based on the notion that there is no one "single" intelligence, but rather a combination. The famous psychologist J. P. Guilford identified some 80 separate abilities that might be considered part of intelligence. These "special factor" tests are usually divided into categories or groups, such as vocabulary, reading comprehension, verbal analogies, spatial relationships, arithmetic reasoning, and so on.

Some of the longer tests, such as the Chicago Test of Primary Mental

Abilities and the SRA Primary Mental Abilities Test, report in terms of subscores or "factors." The Chicago Test, for example, deals with:

N (number): the ability to carry out the basic arithmetic processes.
V (verbal): the understanding of ideas presented verbally.
WF (word fluency): the ability to express oneself in writing or speech.
M (memory): the ability to repeat sequences of words or numbers.
R (reasoning): the ability to solve problems.
S (spatial): the ability to perceive relationships in space.

The catch is that most tests, even those with factor subscores, still report one single score. So, in effect, the subscores don't mean much unless the test is used for diagnostic purposes and low scorers are singled out for remedial work in special areas. But most tests, whether "g" or factor type, are still used to give you a single score—and to classify and screen you rather than to help you.

Most of the tests contain the same general types of items, although not in the same order or format. Some tests organize items in increasing order of difficulty, with the types of items intermingled. Others have factor subsections. Be aware, by the way, that the IQ score you get on one test may not be the same as the IQ you get on another, especially if they're of different types. Also, your scores on verbal and nonverbal tests (those that involve figures, pictures or things, rather than words), or on group and individually administered tests may be quite different.

Below are the more common types of questions you'll find on group verbal tests, together with examples. These may appear in different forms, but here they'll be presented mainly as multiple-choice items.

1. *General Information*
An example of a continent is   (a) the Atlantic   (b) the North Pole
(c) North America   (d) France
Sonatas are created by   (a) authors   (b) conductors   (c) composers
(d) musicians

2. *Vocabulary*
Sanguine means the same as   (a) lacking   (b) hopeful   (c) calm
(d) depressed
Obtuse is the opposite of   (a) stupid   (b) clever   (c) thin   (d) wide

3. *Verbal Analogies*
Quiet is to *noise* as _____ is to _____.
(a) darkness: night   (b) darkness: light   (c) sun: day   (d) rest: sleep
A is to *Z* as *first* is to   (a) second   (b) farthest   (c) oldest   (d) final

4. *Unscrambling Sentences*
To children learn to go school in order
Representations numbers symbolic are

25

5. *Synonyms-Antonyms*
Which word means the *same as* or the *opposite of* the word at the left?
scorch   (a) heat   (b) burn   (c) humid   (d) sizzle
epithet   (a) inscription   (b) description   (c) exclamation
              (d) memorial
maladroit   (a) skillful   (b) intelligent   (c) honest   (d) likeable

6. *Logical Choice*
Paper is commonly used for money because it is   (a) rare   (b) light
(c) durable   (d) counterfeit-proof
Schools must have   (a) principals   (b) students   (c) teachers   (d) tests

7. *Logic and Reasoning*
If the first two statements are true, which other statement *must* also be true?
All mammals are animals. All cats are mammals.
(a) All cats are animals   (b) All mammals are cats   (c) All animals are
mammals   (d) Some cats are animals
All X's are either A, B, or C. This X is not C. Therefore
(a) X is A   (b) X is either A or B   (c) X is B   (d) X is either B or C

8. *Groupings*
Which word does not belong in the group?
(a) apple   (b) pear   (c) carrot   (d) tomato
(a) elm   (b) oak   (c) maple   (d) pine
(a) lake   (b) stream   (c) river   (d) brook

9. *Arithmetic Computation*
$(65 + 24) \times 2 =$ (a) 187   (b) 91   (c) 178   (d) 87
$(24 \times 3) - 3 =$ (a) 78   (b) 72   (c) 24   (d) 69
$18 \div \frac{3}{4} =$ (a) 13½   (b) 12   (c) 24   (d) 13¼

10. *Problems (mathematics)*
If two oranges cost 15 cents, how many oranges can be bought for 75
cents?   (a) 15   (b) 7½   (c) 5   (d) 10
A car travels 15 miles in 20 minutes. How many miles an hour is it
going?   (a) 50   (b) 45   (c) 30   (d) 60
A chain link fence of 550 feet is installed around a property. The cost of
the fence uninstalled is $1.35 a foot. Installed, it costs a total of $1,017.50.
What was the cost per foot for installation?   (a) 20¢   (b) 25¢   (c) 50¢
(d) 75¢

11. *Numerical Series*
What number comes next in each series?
7 21 63 189 567 ?   (a) 1134   (b) 378   (c) 1583   (d) 1701
6 11 9 14 12 17 ?   (a) 15   (b) 18   (c) 19   (d) 22

26

12. *Following Directions*

Cross out the letter below that is the same as the next-to-the-last letter of the fourth word of this sentence.

e   r   o   h

Cross out the even number that is not in a circle and that is unaccompanied by a letter

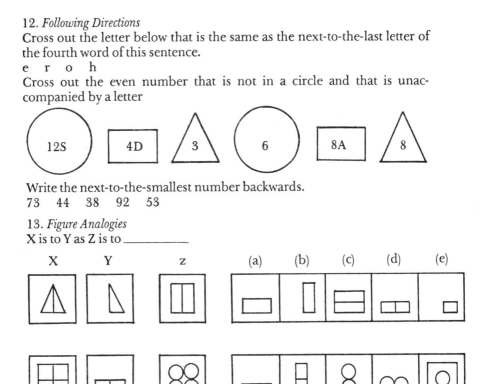

Write the next-to-the-smallest number backwards.

73   44   38   92   53

13. *Figure Analogies*

X is to Y as Z is to _____

14. *Missing or Extra Parts*
Of the following, which picture is most accurate?

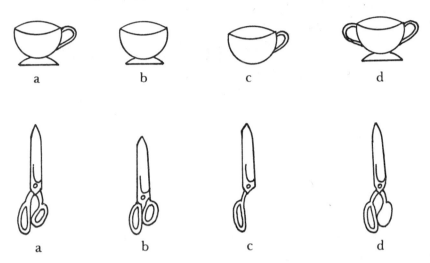

3.
The Mysteries
of Test-Making

Testing and test-taking are major activities in America nowadays; everybody's life is affected by tests. Yet it's surprising how few Americans know much about tests or testing. It's somewhat amusing that so many teachers and professors—who resent and resist the intrusion of outsiders trying to enter their disciplines without proper credentials—assume that test-makers are qualified to give tests, to grade, evaluate, categorize, and screen other people without knowing which side of a bell-shaped curve is up.

The discipline of psychometrics—mental measurement—can become pretty complicated, but the basic ideas are fairly easy to grasp. Because testing and grades are so important to your future, you may be interested in knowing more about the discipline of testing. (This knowledge may not help you to pass tests, though. If that's your only interest in reading this book, you've just finished this chapter.)

MEASUREMENT AND EVALUATION

The terms *measurement* and *evaluation* are often used interchangeably, yet they don't mean the same thing.

When you *measure* something, you're simply comparing it with a standard—an inch, a meter, a pound, a minute, or a degree. Measurement alone tells you nothing about whether the quantity being measured is good or bad, big or little, hot or cold. It just tells you that the page on which you're reading these words is 7 by 9¼ inches, or that it's 67 degrees Fahrenheit outside, or that you got 70% of the questions right on the last math test you took.

But is 70% good or bad? Passing or failing? That depends on another set of standards in which *value judgments* are made about the measurement figures. If your 70% on the math test was the highest score in your class, the chances are it will be *evaluated* as pretty good. But if everybody else in the class got 80's and 90's, you can figure out (even if you aren't very good at math) that you're not going to be evaluated very high.

So in order to *measure* things, you need standards of size or weight or heat or time or achievement. You also need standards by which to *evaluate;* and both involve some kind of comparison. A rather corny joke among psychometricians deals with two test experts who meet on the street. "How's your wife?" asks the first. "Compared with whom?" responds the second.

But evaluation does not mean that you must be compared only with others. For example, your 70% in math might look pretty good if your previous scores had been 40's and 50's. By and large, there are three sets of standards by which you are likely to be evaluated:

• You can be measured against others (perhaps you did better than two-thirds of those who took the test, and not as well as the other third). This score can be turned into an evaluation when the teacher decides what score is passing, or what score is high enough to be converted into an A (*excellent,* from the word *excel,* to surpass others) or low enough to warrant an F. This kind of comparison, in terms of a "norm" or average, is referred to as "normative." (A norm, by the way, is an *average,* not a *standard.* In any population, *half* of the members, more or less, must be above the norm, and half below.)

• You can be measured against a list of "competencies." For example, how many of ten tennis serves do you land in the service court? This measurement, too, becomes an evaluation when it is converted into a judgment. For example, 10 out of 10 may be considered A; 8 out of 10 may be B, and so on. Or 8 out of 10 may mean that you have established your competence on that activity and you may now be sent on to learn backhand returns. Because this kind of evaluation involves clearly defined standards or criteria that are established in advance, it is often referred to as *criterion-referenced.*

• You can be measured against your *own* earlier performance to ascertain how much you've improved or learned. Again, this measurement becomes evaluation when converted into what the powers-that-be have decided is reasonable or adequate.

So *all* evaluation is arbitrary in the sense that somebody has to set up standards for what constitutes "satisfactory" work. Believe it or not, a few schools and teachers don't evaluate. They just measure, and let *you* do the evaluation. But by this time, you've already been conditioned to know what the standards are, or at least to compare yourself with others, which is the usual or common standard.

WHAT IS AVERAGE?

Since we're discussing measuring you against a norm or an average, let's spend a little time on the various meanings of the word. To statisticians, an average is a measure of "central tendency." There are three major ways of thinking of central tendency.

The *mean,* or the *arithmetic mean,* is the kind of average you have used most of your life. It is the sum of the scores divided by the number of cases. When all of the cases are reasonably similar, as when you're averaging your test scores, this kind of average can be useful. But any major discrepancies, or an attempt to compare things that aren't really in the same ballpark, can distort the figures badly. If, for example, we average the income of five retirees chosen at random on a Florida beach, we may find that one man receives $1 million a year from investments while the other four get an "average" of $5,000 a year. For this group as a whole, the "average" income is $204,000—a gross distortion of any given case. A standard joke is that a man may be "statistically" comfortable with one foot on a block of ice and the other in a pot of boiling water.

The *mode,* or the *modal average,* focuses on the score that seems to be the most common in a group. It ignores unusual or skewed items. It is the midpoint of the "interval" that contains the largest number of cases. In the above retirement group, $5,000 would be the modal income.

The *median* is the midpoint in any distribution; half the cases are on one side of it and half the cases are on the other side. The median is often used when the distribution is skewed or lopsided.

Let's take a class test and see how each average works out. Here are the test scores in a class of 31 students:

100% was attained by	2 persons	40% was attained by	0 persons
90%	5	30%	0
80%	6	20%	3
70%	12	10%	0
60%	0	0%	3
50%	0		

The *arithmetic mean* (a total score of 2,030 divided by 31)   = 65%
The *mode* (the largest or "most popular" group)   = 70%
The *median* (15 students from the top, 15 from the bottom)   = 70%

THAT FAMOUS CURVE (ON WHICH YOU MAY BE GRADED)

Practically everybody in school talks knowingly about "grading on the curve." This means that a few students will get A's, far more will get B's and C's, and at least somebody will fail, even if the class is made up of the brightest kids in the school, or the dullest.

The curve is known properly as the "normal curve," or the "normal frequency distribution" or simply the "bell-shaped curve." It is based on the finding that in any random distribution of characteristics (height, or weight, or length of nose) more people are found at the average than at either extreme. More people are of average height than are very tall or very short. If any large-scale random distribution is plotted on a graph, it looks like this, with the stick figures representing the number of people in each category.

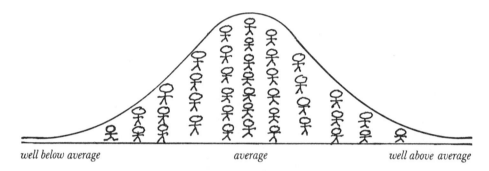

well below average   *average*   *well above average*

Let's take an example of such a distribution in the case of a spelling test of 100 words given to an entire school population of 3,000 students. You'll find several ways in which the information can be reported out.

The distribution is reported first in *raw scores*—the number of words spelled correctly. But raw scores don't tell us much about how students did on the test. Suppose you got 70 words correct. How do you stand in comparison with others?

For comparison purposes, the raw scores must be converted into more meaningful scores. The diagram shows that with 70 words correct, you spelled more words correctly than did 84% of the school population. Another way of putting it is to say that your score was in the 84th percentile. The distribution could also have been reported in *stanines,* based on a 9-unit scale in which a score of 5 is average. Your raw score of 70 would put you in the 7th stanine.

The idea of *standard deviation* probably will not mean much to you, but it means a good deal to the test-maker interested in comparing the performance of several groups of students on the same test, or of the same group of students on different tests. By definition, if we measure off one standard deviation in both directions from the mean, we include approximately 68% of the cases. About two-thirds of the students, then, spelled between 30 and 70 words correctly. The standard deviation provides test-makers with a common system for comparing achievement when different tests or different groups are involved. (And that's probably more than you ever really wanted to know about standard deviation.)

32

Normal distribution curve segments:

| 60 students 2% | 420 students 14% | 1020 students 34% | 1020 students 34% | 420 students 14% | 60 students 2% |

Raw score (number of words spelled correctly)	10	20	30	40	50	60	70	80	90
Number of students scoring at or below each raw score	70		480		1500		2520		2931
Percent scoring at or below each raw score	2.3%		15.9%		50%		84%		97.7%
Standard deviation	−2.0		−1.0		0		+1.0		+2.0
Stanines	← 1	2	3	4	5	6	7	8	9 →
Percent in each stanine	4%	7%	12%	17%	20%	17%	12%	7%	4%

So far we've been talking about measurement alone, not evaluation. How "good" is your score of 70 words correct out of 100? Making value judgments usually involves converting these measurement units into *grades* of some sort—A, B, C, D, and F, for example, or "excellent" to "unsatisfactory." In large populations, like the student population of a school or college, the distribution will probably be distributed in a "normal" manner, with the majority of students getting C's (although with the "grade inflation" of recent years, this normal grade is moving into the B range) and smaller proportions getting either A's or F's.

A lot of teachers deliberately grade on the curve, with the top 7 to 10 percent getting A's, say, and the lowest 7 to 10 percent getting F's. Most students will get grades in the average ranges. Even a little thought makes it clear that in a small group like a class, grading on the curve doesn't make much sense. For one thing, it means that students in a pretty sharp class can end up with D's for work that would have earned B's in another class. Furthermore, college admissions officers look at grades, without considering whether you got them in honors classes or not. Where teachers grade on the curve, your grade is determined more by the kind of class in which you find yourself than by what *you* actually achieve.

Why do so many teachers and professors grade on the curve? Simple—it gives the appearance of "objectivity." Anything the teacher does, or doesn't do, won't matter. Even if he or she mumbled all term and gave the exam in Sanskrit, grading on the curve will result in a normal distribution, relieving the teacher of the responsibility of thinking through instruction or of establishing meaningful standards for evaluation.

Most experts agree that grading on the curve is a monstrosity. But it does help teachers stay out of trouble with administrators, most of whom don't like to see too many A's or F's in a class. And it does make life easier: avoiding the establishment of reasonable standards, says one textbook on tests and measurements, may be comforting to the teacher "in that he can avoid soul-searching about the fairness of particular grades, but the system gives little or no information relevant to planning further instruction." And Dr. Benjamin Bloom of the University of Chicago thinks that grading on a curve will also convince the majority of our students that they can't possibly learn well no matter what they do. There is nothing sacred about the normal distribution, say Bloom and his colleagues. "It is the distribution most appropriate to chance and random activity," they declare, but "education is a purposeful activity, and we seek to have the students learn what we have to teach. . . . In fact, we may even insist that our educational efforts have been *unsuccessful* to the extent that the distribution of achievement approximates the normal. . . ."

But some teachers, and professors, and administrators are slow learners. So if you're in a class where the teacher grades on the curve, do your best to get out. (Unless it's a very dull class and you figure that *you're* bound to get the A—and if you're willing to risk brain rot for the sake of a good grade.)

SOME COMMON WORDS WITH UNCOMMON MEANINGS

Most teacher-made tests are not only badly conceived, but badly engineered. They're full of errors, clues, and giveaways. As a result, they may be easy to beat, even if you don't know much about a subject. (A later chapter will deal with taking these tests.)

But there's a large group of tests made up by experts. These are the so-called *standardized* tests, the kind you see when you take an IQ test or an SAT or any achievement test distributed by one of the large companies that sells tests commercially. These tests are bought by schools and companies because they're *standardized,* they've been *validated,* their *reliability* has been authenticated, and they're *objective.* And what you think those words mean in your dictionary or in conversation has little to do with what they mean to psychometricians.

First of all, let's look at what these words *don't* mean in test-making. When test-makers call a test *objective,* they don't mean that no personal judgments are built into the test. When they say a test is *reliable,* they don't mean it can be relied upon. And when they say a test is *valid,* they don't mean that the results are meaningful. The words are used in a special technical sense.

Objectivity: A test is objective if the same standards or conditions of testing apply to everybody who takes the test, and if everybody is graded by the same standards. Objectivity, to test-makers, really means *uniformity*: your test score doesn't depend on whether the teacher likes you, or has a headache that morning, or got a speeding ticket last night. If choice (c) is correct for that pretty redhead in the front row, it has to be correct for you.

You've probably taken enough tests to know that essay tests, by and large, are not very objective. A teacher or professor marking essay tests in the morning is not likely to apply the same standards that he or she will apply late in the afternoon or late at night—or the next morning, or the next term. And the same answer might receive a much higher or lower grade from another teacher or prof.

Objective test items have only *one* correct answer. The rub is that a test question can be objective and still be a bad question. It can be a terrible, stupid, and nonsensical question. For example:

How tall is tall enough?   (a) taller than you   (b) taller than three giraffes (c) as tall as the Empire State Building   (d) three stories high

All the test-maker has to do to keep this question objective is to be sure that everybody who marks (c) correct—and only these persons—is given credit for that answer. So objectivity alone is no guarantee of a good question. Some test experts, in fact, think that objectivity can even be a bad thing in testing. It can minimize the application of imagination, creativity, or even advanced knowledge. It can penalize the test-taker who knows too much or who reads into the question—or the answers—things that the test-maker did not intend.

But objectivity does two things: it makes tests easier to score and grade (often by machine) and it provides for more uniform, but not necessarily more reasonable, marking standards.

35

Standardization: The key to comparing individual performances is to have everybody perform "standard tasks." Standardized testing is usually *normative*; its main purpose, usually, is to help teachers, administrators, employers, and others to compare people. Standardization involves the conversion of raw scores, like the number of correct answers on a test, into units for comparison, like percentiles or stanines or quartiles (you guessed it—same idea but with four categories). Stanines and quartiles, in contrast to percentiles, avoid the appearance of precision because they present a *range* rather than an apparently precise score.

But these normative standardized tests can tell you how well you do *only* in comparison with others. They can't and don't tell anyone what *you* know or how *you* think. And the word "standard" relates only to the population of test-takers, not to criteria or standards for judging performance.

Let's say you get back your standardized test scores—usually in a computerized printout—and they tell you that you achieved in the 70th percentile. One thing that *doesn't* mean is that the scores of everybody who took the test at the time you did were dumped into a computer and the relative standings and rankings were worked out. So where did they get the norms and the percentile figures? They got it by comparing you with a *standardization sample,* or model group, that the test-makers *thought* represented a fair cross section of the kind of people who would take the test. If the test-makers were accurate, the scores of the sample population will represent the scores that would have been obtained if all the millions of students in the country had been tested. If they were wrong in their estimation of what makes a fair cross section, the reported scores will be biased. Obviously, some companies that publish tests are more accurate than others in their establishment of a standardization sample.

Reliability: This is a word that test-makers use a good deal, mainly because it can be calculated fairly accurately. A tremendous amount of the literature sent out by the testing companies—to you, to school officials, to university admissions officers—make a big thing of reliability. But the importance of reliability in a test can easily be overstated, and the figures used can be misleading.

Reliability in testing means that *a test agrees with itself.* If you take a test today and then take it a week from now (and let's assume that you had learned nothing from actually taking the test the first time) you should get the same score the second time. To put it another way, a reliable test is consistent in its results.

Reliability can be measured in a number of ways. The *test-retest* approach mentioned in the last paragraph has some built-in problems, as you may already have figured out. For one thing, people who have taken a test once *do* learn something. They learn something about the test itself, and most people do acquire additional information between the first test and the retest. Some companies give "equivalent" or "parallel" forms of the same test to see if the results are consistent. Or they split the test into two halves, perhaps by calling the odd-numbered questions one half and the even-numbered questions the other, to see if the grades on each half match. In any case, if the test is reliable, your score on one test should be pretty much the same as on the other. In this way, the test-makers can be pretty sure that whatever the test is measuring, it's being consistent in measuring it.

The more reliable the test, the higher the "coefficient of reliability," and the more likely it is that you'd get the same score on a retest. For a standardized achievement test, a reliability coefficient of .95 is considered excellent; .90 is acceptable; and .80 is a bit shaky. But test-makers can do some pretty tricky things to boost reliability coefficients artificially. One way is to cut time limits. Let's assume that we give a word definition test of 100 words to a class of students all of whom *can* define the words. However, because we allow a 15-minute time limit, only a few students can finish the list; most get about three-quarters of the list done; some get only about halfway through. On a retest with the same time limit, we're likely to get the same results, with the faster writers getting higher scores. So while we may think we're testing for the ability to define words, we may actually be testing for speed.

But no matter how reliable a test may be, there is a built-in chance of variation as a result of the test itself, the way you feel that day, and the presence of distractions. So it isn't very likely that you'll get exactly the same score on a test and retest, or on parallel forms or on split halves. Thus a statistical concept of "standard error" is used to estimate the range, the possible "deviation" or error from your "true score." This standard error is closely connected with the reliability of the test: the higher the reliability, the lower the standard error.

Let's see what standard error can mean by considering the 1974 edition of a widely used junior high school achievement test, usually taken at the end of the seventh grade. The publisher's manual for this test lists a standard error for the language section as 3.9. In the words of the manual, "We could expect with about 68% certainty that the true score" for a student with a raw score of 43 would fall between 39 and 47. According to the test's conversion table, this means a spread between the 44th percentile (below average) and the 60th percentile (above average). Put another way, the spread in "grade equivalency" ranges from two months into the seventh grade (7.2) to nine months into the eighth grade (8.9). In this particular test, a difference of *two questions* right or wrong could, in some cases, result in an error of *a year and a half* in the reported grade level of achievement.

Even with the most carefully designed tests such as the SAT, there is a chance of error, although it is much less than in the test reported above. With the test publishers themselves admitting a built-in possibility of error in the reported scores, isn't it fascinating how some college admissions officers will deny otherwise good candidates on the basis of one or two percentile points below a cut-off point?

Validity: This is the heart and soul of a test or a testing program. Validity is the degree to which a test measures what it is supposed to measure. Obviously, unless a test is valid for its purpose, it's useless, even if it's standardized, objective, and reliable.

But establishing a test's validity can be pretty tricky. How do we know that a test measures what it's supposed to? One way is simply to ask experts in the subject to examine the test and agree that it does. Do they think that the items all deal with the test's basic purpose? That it is a pretty good sampling of what testers call "the universe of tasks"? (Obviously, nobody can test you on "math" or "French"; you can be tested only on a sampling of different kinds of math problems, and of words and phrases in French.) This kind of validity is called *face validity* or *content validity*. A more accurate description would be "validity by opinion." But of course publishers would rather claim that a test "possesses a high content validity" than say that "the people we asked to look at the test think it's pretty good."

Actually, there's nothing wrong with validation by opinion. As Robert L. Ebel, former vice-president of ETS, points out: "Inspection is the means used to validate a diamond, the books of a business, or the title to a property. Why some test specialists insist it is inappropriate to validate an achievement by inspection is hard to understand." The problem, of course, is that lots of people out there are going to make decisions about your future on the assumption that these impressive statistics and figures somehow legitimize the test's content validity. They might be a lot less certain if they knew precisely what "content validity" means.

For the tests we're talking about, another kind of validity—criterion validity—is established by comparing the test with something else that we think measures what the test is supposed to measure. For example, we can give a test to measure a construct such as "an understanding of historical principles." And those who scored highest in the test were also those who got the highest grades in history classes. Doesn't this correlation establish the criterion validity of the test?

Not necessarily. Suppose that in fact, the history test emphasized memorization, as many history tests do, instead of an understanding of historical principles. And suppose that many history teachers *also* focus on the memorization of names, dates, and statements to be recited back. Or, suppose that the test in math that claims to measure an understanding of mathematical principles really focuses on simple computational skills, as most math tests do. And suppose that the teacher, as many math teachers do, emphasizes simple manipulation of numbers.

In these examples, the tests are not valid in terms of the construct they *claim* to measure, or in terms of what teachers may *think* the test is measuring, although they may be valid in terms of what the teachers are actually teaching. If we really want to measure an understanding of *principles,* then we have to establish another criterion. Or we can go back to the experts in history or math for another round of opinion validation. Or we can do what a lot of schools and teachers actually do: keep right on using the tests in the belief that they measure what they don't. You might find it interesting to visit a college library and look up a copy of Buros' *Mental Measurements Yearbook,* the Bible of the testing industry, and glance at the reviews of the tests by some of the country's leading experts. There are quite a few achievement, personality, and aptitude tests being sold every year (and bought, presumably, by schools that manipulate their students' futures based on their results) that Buros' reviewers don't consider very valid in terms of what they promise and what the schools think they're getting.

Probably the most accurate way of establishing a test's validity is by verifying—as one textbook on testing puts it—its ability "to predict something other than itself." If a pre-employment test promises to measure a worker's ability to perform on the job to his supervisors' satisfaction, then the test is valid if the workers who got high scores also get good evaluations from their supervisors. Most scholastic aptitude tests like the SAT, GRE, and LSAT claim to predict the likelihood that applicants will perform successfully (get good grades) in colleges or graduate or professional schools. How well do they do this? According to some experts, not as well as many school counselors and college admissions officers think. We'll come back to the question of predictive validity in another chapter.

Thus, a test can be objective, standardized, reliable, and valid, and still be a pretty bad test. But most tests are *not* very reliable or valid. According to a three-volume guide produced by a research group at UCLA, "far less than 10%" of the tests studied were given "good" grades. Ralph Hoepfner, head of the project, defends the better tests but he admits that "there's a lot of 'schlock' on the market."

And Oscar Buros warns that "the best of our tests are still highly fallible instruments which are extremely difficult to interpret with assurance in individual cases."

But many school counselors, admissions officers, parents, and students don't believe the experts—or at least don't act as if they believe them.

You can believe them.

4.
General Strategies
of Test-Taking

By this time, it should be pretty obvious that tests don't always measure what they're supposed to—whether it be intelligence, personality, success on the job, or even your understanding of a subject. But whatever they do measure, tests can help you or hurt you throughout your school career and vocational life. After all, classroom tests are the major source of information for the determination of school grades; and standardized tests provide the data base on which decisions are made to admit you or keep you out of special classes, graduate programs, professional schools, and an increasing number of jobs.

As far as test-taking skills are concerned, there are some important differences between the professionally made standardized tests and the teacher-made classroom tests; we'll deal with specifics of each in later chapters. But there are some important similarities, too. The first one is based on the recognition that it is possible to *learn how to take tests.*

EFFECTIVE PREPARATION

Despite the rhetoric, most tests are *not* used to help you unless you're in a particularly good school and have exceptionally sensitive teachers.* In fact, a lot of money and effort have gone into the preparation of tests to beat you. This book focuses on helping you to beat the test. But this doesn't promise a set of fast, easy gimmicks. People don't make fortunes in the stock market or in real estate (or in gambling, for that matter) by playing hunches, trusting to luck, or relying on a few tricks; the key in each of these activities is careful analysis, thorough preparation, and skillful operation. A few tricks or gimmicks don't hurt, but they're not enough. Skillful test-taking isn't very different.

We're not going to sermonize here, but you probably have heard or read some of these tips before and, if you're like most people, you haven't bothered taking them seriously. You should. Cumulative experience shows that they do help.

Begin early. If you're concerned about class tests, start the first day of the class.

Study regularly. Whether it be exercise, dieting, playing tennis, or studying, any activity becomes more effective if it's made a habit and a way of life. Study every day or every other day, not when you feel like it or when you're inspired. Preferably, it should be under the same conditions, in the same room—even at the same time of day, if possible. Such routines reinforce the habitual nature of regular studying. Start with the most difficult subjects so you're working on these when you're fresh; resist the temptation to put off the work you consider unpleasant. Take breaks—but schedule them. Otherwise, it's too tempting to decide you're ready for a break when you run into a snag.

"Overstudy." Don't stop studying when you think you understand the material. Research shows that being better prepared than you think you have to be pays dividends—up to a point. At this "point of diminishing returns," the amount of overstudying doesn't give you enough more to warrant the extra time. As a rule of thumb, when you think you're ready, put in another 25% of the time you've already spent.

---

*This passage provoked Dr. John W. French to write in the margin of my manuscript: "Discuss the *real* reasons that people use tests—admissions officers: to achieve a homogeneous student body or avoid problems; teachers: to motivate study and to evaluate work in order to maintain standards; employers: to secure effective workers so that they can make a profit."

I agree that these are among the reasons tests are used. But I maintain that they have little to do with helping *you*. They are designed to help institutions, administrators, teachers, and employers. And I'm not sure that they always help *them*. I don't believe that "homogenized" colleges and universities promote the cross-fertilization of ideas or the intellectual nonconformity that promotes creative thinking. In my view, such institutions are dedicated to what Fishman and Clifford call "the pursuit of the standard mind and the standard man." And I think that for employers to depend on standardized pencil-and-paper tests to evaluate on-the-job ability is like calling the weather bureau to learn if it's raining outside.

Some tests are reward-oriented, like the CLEP (College Level Examination Program), for example, or the New York State Regents Scholarship Examination. But most tests, in my view, are designed to classify you, not to help you—to keep the gates open only to those who conform. People like Edison and Einstein—notoriously poor test-takers—might not make it today.

Review previous exams and quizzes. You're not likely to find the same questions that you'll get on your exam—although this has been known to happen, especially on classroom exams. But instructors have their individual approaches and methods of operation. (One of the most effective tools of police work is the analysis of a criminal's *modus operandi* [M.O.] in order to anticipate his moves.) You should be able to analyze the testing techniques and styles that you can expect. (Incidentally, knowing the *form* of test in advance—multiple-choice or completion or essay—doesn't seem to make as much difference as many students think.)

Organize your studying. Analysis of past tests helps you to figure out whether to emphasize facts or ideas, major principles or trivia. But the general approach to studying should deal with basics. Start by getting an overview—of a chapter, a book, a lecture. Note the main ideas; it might pay to turn them into questions that you proceed to answer. Summarize the ideas, both main ideas and supporting data. You can do this by taking notes, or by making notes in the margin of your textbook or notebook. Or you can underline the main ideas, especially if the author provides a summary section for each group of related thoughts. A recent study showed that students who took notes on a textbook passage performed better on tests than those who merely underlined, especially if they didn't know what kind of test to expect. In turn, those who underlined did better than those who merely read the material. The experimenters suggested that it may have been the increase in study time that helped the students to raise their grades.

Review periodically. At least once a week, review your notes and your books. If you've taken notes on lectures, summarize them in a sort of index on the margin of the page, noting the major facts and the relationship between the facts. Don't just *list* topics, though: summarize major ideas, findings, and conclusions. This procedure is one of the major exercises in successful studying. Review your notes frequently.

Cram intelligently. Those all-night sessions generally do more harm than good. Staggering into an examination at nine in the morning, bleary-eyed and mind-boggled, isn't the best way to approach the exam. The major reason for such sessions is fairly obvious: they're an attempt to cram a whole term's work into a few hours. And they're an admission that you're not really comfortable with your grasp of the subject. On the other hand, if you have studied regularly, an intensive review is a good preparation, especially if you work at summarizing and making sense out of your notes.

ANALYZE THE TEST SITUATION

Before you walk into the test room, you should have a general idea of what to expect. Does that sound impossible? Good test-takers do it all the time, even if they're not always aware of the process.

Have you taken this teacher's tests before? If so, you have an idea about the kinds of tests he or she gives. Are they straight memorization? In this case, you'll have to go through your notes or your textbook to pick up *key phrases, words,* and *ideas*. Usually, it isn't necessary to memorize everything, unless the teacher is a sadist who delights in trapping students (unfortunately, there are a few of these around). Most standardized tests focus on application of basic principles and concepts. Teacher-made examinations can run the gamut. And believe it or not, you're much better off in a class where the teacher gives quizzes and tests frequently. This kind of situation helps you to know what to expect in the big tests. The teacher who seldom gives tests is being unfair on a number of levels. First of all, your grade is more likely to depend on just one or a few big tests. Second, you're not able to analyze the teacher's style and expectations until it may be too late.

If you have a teacher who gives tests infrequently, try to get information from former students who have taken this teacher's tests. Don't ask for specific questions—that's a sucker play *unless* this teacher is known for giving the same test over and over. In most cases, the questions have changed—remember the old joke, "Just when I learned the answers, they changed the questions"? It's more important to learn the teacher's *style*. The M.O. isn't as likely to change.

In general, after the first test in any class, analyze what happened: What kinds of questions were asked? What was the thrust? Were trivia or basics emphasized? Was the test based on memorization or the application of major principles? On abstractions or concrete situations? The answers to these questions should help you to know how to prepare for the future tests.

Become familiar with standardized test directions and formats well ahead of time. Most of the big test publishers distribute information in advance that tells you how the test is designed, gives you basic test instructions, explains the scoring methods, and may even provide samples of test questions for you to practice with. Examine these carefully; you can't assume that all test instructions or formats are the same. But by the same token, don't put blind faith in these familiarization brochures and booklets. A reviewer of the College English Placement Exam wrote in the *Mental Measurement Yearbook* that "It does not help when two of the three sample exercises presented to 'familiarize yourself with the kinds of items in the test' are not in the test in that form." And if you're practicing from old exams—a great idea—be aware that some basic directions change from time to time. So read and practice—but when you go into the examination room, be prepared to find variations.

HOW IMPORTANT ARE ENVIRONMENTAL VARIABLES?

There's no clear-cut answer. Although anxiety can be a block to effective test-taking, there's some evidence that many people actually do better under a degree of stress, *short* of the nausea, upset-stomach, and headache variety. Some research indicates that with many test-takers, nervousness just makes their test scores more unpredictable, not necessarily lower. A study by Dr. John W. French of ETS indicated that anxiety has little effect on the scores of students taking a college entrance examination. Interestingly enough, older people can easily be thrown by nervousness, and tranquilizers can help them score higher. But tranquilizers don't seem to help most younger test-takers. In fact, the use of any kind of drug may actually handicap them by interfering with their judgment.

A lot of the bull-session wisdom suggests all-night cram sessions. These may work for some people, but most people can do considerably better after a good night's sleep, especially on tests that emphasize thought rather than rote recitation. For tests that do stress memorization, on the other hand, cramming can help, but not to the point where you're half asleep during the test. As a general rule, do whatever cramming you want to do beforehand, and save the last night for sleep.

Don't underestimate the value of physical well-being. Research indicates that some women don't do well just before their menstrual periods. If you have a choice on such situations, try to postpone the test if you're not well or if you're overwrought.

In any case, light, regular exercise before the test can help greatly. Just before taking the test, try to relax physically. From your feet up, consciously relax your muscles, one group at a time. If you're familiar with the techniques of progressive relaxation, this would be a good time to apply some modified versions. Slow down your breathing and breathe deeply as you wait.

USE YOUR TIME INTELLIGENTLY

In terms of time allowed, there are two kinds of tests: *speed tests*, in which you're given a limited amount of time, and *power tests*, where your ability to perform the tasks is considered more important than the speed with which you perform them.

Speed tests are given for two basic reasons, one legitimate and the other somewhat dishonest. The legitimate reason is based on the assumption that the speed with which you perform is an indication of how well you've learned a subject—an assumption, by the way, that isn't universally accepted. The dishonest reason is that a test's reliability coefficient can be boosted by limiting the time: the greater the speed requirements, the higher the reliability coefficient will be. In other words, faster test-takers will be faster every time they take a test, so the comparative results are based in large part on speed rather than on the ability to do the tasks.

In a sense, all tests are timed. Even in the most liberal power test, there's a time when the proctors are ready to leave and the janitors are ready to clean up. As a rule of thumb, 80% of the test takers should complete a good power test. So if you want high scores, you'll have to allocate your time wisely.

On standardized tests, you'll usually be told how long you have to work on each section. Once you're finished with a section, there's normally no going back. If no time is indicated for each section, you'll have to make your own determination. In any case, the time you spend on each question should be calculated.

Review the test and set up your own schedule. In a highly speeded test (for example, 100 true-false items in a 50-minute class period), you won't have much time for reviewing answers, and you'll simply figure out how much time you have for each item. By mid-period, you should be halfway through. In a classroom test that includes short-answer items and essay questions, divide up the time according to the percentage that each answer will contribute to your total grade. If the essays count for 40% of the grade, allocate about 40% of the time. Unless the test is highly speeded, allow some time for review and for going back to the items you omitted the first time through. If you're proceeding too fast, it could mean that you're doing great; but it might mean that you're committing a classic low-scorer goof: guessing instead of reasoning through the tough items.

Work the easier items first, in order to gain as many points as possible in the time allotted. Then go back to the tougher items. Be sure to keep a record of the items you skipped. Keep in mind that many standardized tests are organized from easy to hard within each category. If you see that this is the case, just work straight through as quickly as you can without sacrificing accuracy.

Summary:
- Skim the test.
- Set up a schedule.
- Guess or leave out harder questions; mark them for return.
- Use time remaining to review and reconsider answers.

HOW IMPORTANT ARE TEST INSTRUCTIONS?

There's no one answer to this question, but *in general*, test instructions are very important. Study after study has shown that one outstanding deficiency among low scorers is their failure to pay enough attention to instructions. In the words of one study, poor test-takers "were easily sidetracked." Most rush through instructions in order to get to the questions themselves, which they promptly foul up because, having failed to note important details, they don't do what they're told. For example, some test instructions ask you to choose a multiple-choice item that does *not* fit a category; low scorers frequently choose the first alternative that *does* fit because that is what they *expect* to be asked.

Let's look over the shoulder of John B., an unsuccessful college problem solver in a well-known study by Bloom and Broder, *The Problem-Solving Processes of College Students*.

Problem: Some economists feel that there is danger of an extreme inflationary boom... It is the opinion of such economists that the government should control the boom in order to prevent a depression...

Below are a number of specific suggestions. For each of the following items, blacken

  answer space 1—if it would be *consistent* with the policy of controlling the boom;
  answer space 2—if it is directly *inconsistent* with the policy.

[Three choices followed]
John (thinking aloud as he had been instructed to do):
(Read first item.) "No."
(Read second item.) "Think about that."
(Read third item.) "No—must be [the second one], by the process of elimination."

By skimming the instructions, John converted the task to selecting one of three statements, which is what he *expected* the instructions to ask him to do.

Even if you're not a low scorer, spend enough time on the instructions to know precisely what you have to look for and to do. Never assume that instructions for one part of a test will apply to other parts, or that the instructions for the old tests you practiced on will apply to this one. It might pay for you to underline or circle the key words or phrases, or even to summarize them on the side of the paper. And don't assume that all the questions in the same section will ask you to do the same things. For example:

Which choice means the same as the word at the left?

mutual: (a) unilateral (b) common (c) distinct (d) sundered

Which choice means the opposite of the word at the left?

mendacious: (a) honest (b) deceitful (c) disingenuous (d) begging

Another major problem among low scorers is confusing the answer that the question *itself* calls for and the answer that the test-taker thinks *should* be asked for. For example:

Directions: In each of the following items, you are presented with two statements and four conclusions. In each case, assume that the statements are true. Which one of the conclusions must logically follow?
Statements:
A large brain indicates superior intelligence.
Chinese have larger brains than white Americans.
Conclusions:
(a) Chinese are more intelligent than white Americans.
(b) White Americans cannot score high in Chinese IQ tests.
(c) There is no proven relationship between brain size and intelligence.
(d) Intelligence is a result of genetic and environmental factors.
(e) None of the above conclusions follows.

Obviously, the correct answer is (a), *based on the statements*. But in one research study, it was found that low scorers would often miss this kind of question because, disregarding the directions, they choose answers with which they *agree*. One low-scoring student reported, "Answer A is the one that logically follows, but C is the one I believe, so I took C." Read the question as it is *presented*; don't read into it what you expect to find, or think *should* be.

Withall, Dr. Masha Rudman of the University of Massachusetts, who instructs teachers and school administrators in raising pupil test scores on standardized examinations, advocates "a healthy disrespect for the rules" in some specific respects. On reading-comprehension passages, for example, she suggests that you disregard the usual instructions to "read the passage carefully before answering any of the questions," but instead read the questions first, *before* reading the passage. Many of the tests, she says, measure skim-and-match skills more than comprehension. So don't get too involved in the content or meaning of a passage before you know what is about to be asked of you. There are several kinds of reading-comprehension questions, and recognizing the differences can help you to answer them correctly, while you save time. In a later chapter we'll deal specifically with reading-comprehension questions.

Be skeptical, too, about accepting some of the instructions that deal with guessing. Some instructions approach dishonesty. For example, here is what one *Mental Measurements Yearbook* reviewer writes about a widely used test:

> The student instructions for the TAP battery include the admonition: "If you have no idea whatsoever *about the answer, omit the exercise on the answer sheet.*" In other words, leave it blank. Yet no penalty is levied for wrong answers, and the student who follows this instruction will [on the average] lower his score compared with the next student who, wisely or cynically, disregards it. Furthermore, in applying the suggested rule, a student will often be too self-critical. He may not "think" he knows the answer, but he might be able to eliminate one or two competing alternatives, in which case his chance of raising his score would be even better than chance.
>
> A study of the norms reveals just how much guessing can accomplish. Let us assume a student "knows" enough answers to reach the 48th percentile on the 9th grade norms and then "blindly" guesses the rest. He will, by disregarding the instruction and by guessing only with average luck, raise his performance to the 90th percentile—a gain of 42 percentile points! ... By their instruction, then, the test publishers seem to be penalizing students for obedience.

So, *if* you know what you're asked to do, use your judgment about reading a passage carefully before answering questions or about quessing (there is more about guessing in the next section). But know *why* you're disregarding instructions, if you choose to do so.

Summary:
- Read the instructions carefully; understand what is wanted.
- Answer what is asked of you, not what you think *should* be asked.

- Read the *questions* carefully; don't jump to conclusions.
- Some of the key words and terms in short-answer tests:
  the *same* as; the *opposite* of; *similar* to; *assume* that; *only one* correct choice; *all* the correct choices; if . . . ; all units of measurement (time, space, amount) —these may appear in different forms in the question and the answers, or in several of the answers (feet and inches, dollars and cents, hours and minutes)—convert if necessary.

SHOULD YOU GUESS?

Before you decide whether or not to guess, read the instructions. You can't assume that all short-answer tests are the same. For example, many tests will instruct you to answer all the questions. If this is the case, then by all means guess, because there is no penalty for guessing.

Intelligent guessing, by the way, does not mean tossing a coin or stabbing wildly at an answer. It *does* mean applying logic and looking for contextual clues and, if these don't work, probing for the flaws and giveaways in the test construction. (Test construction clues most often appear in teacher-made classroom tests, and they are listed in Chapter 5; many of them can be found in standardized tests, though). Wild guessing is the *last* resort; low scorers habitually use it as a standard approach.

You should also guess if the instructions tell you that only correct answers will be counted, or if they don't say anything at all about the matter. However, you should be aware that in some tests (such as the SAT and GRE), a percentage of the wrong answers is subtracted from the number of right answers as a penalty for haphazard guessing. In such exams, wild guessing may actually lower your score, and this is where low scorers often go wrong. Usually the instructions will tell you if you are taking a test of this sort, or on the answer sheet you will find a space for tallying the number of wrong answers. Even on such tests, though, it might be to your advantage to guess. If you are not sure of the specifics, but have a general knowledge of the question area, you can usually eliminate one or two of the responses as wrong; you may be able to narrow the choices below the penalty odds.

The idea of penalty is based on the fact that you *could* gain credit by guessing alone. On a four-alternative multiple-choice question, you stand a one-in-four chance of hitting the right answer; and you will probably get one correct out of four such questions. So the penalty is levied against the three you got wrong—probably ⅓ point for each. Assuming each answer is worth 1 point, the formula for figuring the credit you could earn from pure guesswork is:

(probability of being right) + (1 − that probability) × (penalty)

So, on that four-choice question:

Where there is no penalty: ¼ + (1 − ¼) (0) = ¼ + 0 = ¼. Guess, of course!
Where there is a penalty of ¼ point: ¼ + (1 − ¼) (−¼) = ¼ −³/₁₆ = ¹/₁₆. Worth a guess.

Where there is a penalty of ⅓ point: ¼ + (1 − ¼) (−⅓) = 0.
Where there is a penalty of ⅓ point, but you can eliminate one choice:
⅓ + (1 −⅓) (−⅓) = ⅓ − ²/₉ = ¹/₉. Definitely worth a guess.
Where there is a penalty of ½ point: ¼ + (1 − ¼) (−½) = −⅛. Don't guess.

Some multiple-choice tests have "weighted" responses: one choice may be worth 1 point, another may be worth 2 points, a third may be worth 3 points. In such cases, since no response at all means a 0, guessing is very much in order.

In general, the odds are very much in favor of guessing—*after you've used all the test-taking hints in this book.*

Summary:

- Guess when there is no penalty.
- Guess when you have more to gain than to lose.
- Guess if you can eliminate enough options to put the odds in your favor.

SHOULD YOU WHIZ THROUGH?

Not all tests are the same, but for most mass tests a whiz-through approach is a good idea. First of all, skim through the test to get an idea of the kinds of questions that are asked. Does the test demand memory of details and trivia? Or does it call for knowledge of basic principles? While it's too late to go back to restudy, knowing the focus can help you in deciding how to answer many of the questions. In addition, it's surprising how often you may find clues in one question that can help you in answering others. A skimming through also lets you know how to allot your time during the examination.

You should usually work the easier items first and then go back to the harder ones if you have time. A hint: if you're permitted to mark the question sheets, mark with some symbol the questions you want to go back to, so that you don't miss them or waste time checking your blanks on the answer sheet to find them—blanks can be very easy to overlook later. If you can't mark the questions, keep a list by number on a scrap of paper and mark them off as you answer them. If you're taking a machine-scored standardized test, *don't* mark the answer sheet next to the blanks; the scoring machine may pick up such marks as incorrect answers.

FIGURE OUT THE TEST-MAKER'S INTENT

It has been emphasized that low scorers often read into directions or questions what they want or expect to find, rather than what the test actually asks. But students who know *too* much can also fall into the trap of reading into a question what the test-maker didn't intend. An apparent oversimplification may or may *not* be a trap. How can you tell? From your knowledge of the teacher, from your review of previous tests in that class or of that type, from the other items on the test. What degree of sophistication is expected? How important to the answer is the detail that was omitted, or the detail that modifies the question? How important is that extra phrase, in terms of what the test-maker obviously intended? For example:

Napoleon, born of Corsican peasant stock, became First Consul of France in 1799. T F

If you happen to know that Napoleon's father was a village lawyer, not a peasant, should you mark the item *false?* Not unless you have reason to think that the teacher is out to trap students on trivia. Normally, though, on a composite statement—where more than one thought or idea is stated—if one element is *obviously* false, the whole statement is false. For example:

The Empire State Building is in New York City, the capital of New York State. T F

In this case, the substatement that New York City is the capital of New York State is so patently and obviously false that it must be considered a misstatement clearly intended to trap the unwary.

But how do you handle the *missing* statement—the modifying substatement that is needed to make the full statement true?

Water boils at 212 degrees. T F

Is this a trap? The statement doesn't mention whether the degrees are Fahrenheit or Centigrade. Or whether the water is adulterated. Or at sea level. In a case like this, you'll have to figure out the intent of the test-maker from the other information at hand and the nature of the test itself. In many cases, a statement that might be true in an introductory freshman class may be false in an advanced class in the same subject.

An exam, by the way, is not the place to get cute or show off your knowledge; your ego gratification can cost you points, especially on items that are too subtle to be picked up by the average test-taker and that probably weren't considered in the first place. For example:

Thomas Jefferson, who wrote the Declaration of Independence, was the third president of the United States. T F

Now, because you've just read an historical novel, you know that Jefferson wrote the *first* draft of the Declaration, but that there were four other members of the committee assigned to the task, and all had a hand in the final document. Should you mark the item false? The chances are strong that nobody else in the class could know the item of information you've picked up, and that the test-maker didn't intend for it to be considered. So marking this item false could cost you points. But if you sincerely think there's an ambiguity, answer the question as you *think* the teacher or test-maker wanted, and make a note alongside with your qualification or reason for answering as you did. Your comment may be picked up, and you don't lose anything if it isn't.

Summary:
- Normally, one false substatement invalidates a statement.
- Consider the level of sophistication of the test.
- Ascertain the intent of the test-maker.
- Ask the proctor or teacher to clarify ambiguities (if you can).

REASONING THROUGH TO AN ANSWER

In another chapter we'll deal with guessing on the basis of test flaws and mechanical clues, which are quite common on teacher-made tests. Professionals are much better at the mechanics of test-making, although many standardized tests are full of such flaws as well.

In Bloom and Broder's famous study, low scorers and high scorers differed in the way they reasoned through a problem. "The major difference," says the report, "was in the degree to which their approach to the problem might be characterized as active or passive." Low scorers, you may remember:

- assume that they either "know" or "don't know" an answer;
- operate on hunches or feelings;
- give up quickly if a solution is not at hand;
- try to remember solutions to similar problems, rather than solve each new problem independently; and
- use a negative approach, selecting an answer *only* because the others appear unattractive.

High scorers, on the other hand, approach each problem as a challenge, formulate a clear procedure of attack, and set up clear standards and criteria.

Two important findings are worth noting. Many unsuccessful test-takers would begin their attack on a problem much the same way as the high scorers, would reason through part-way—*and would give up too soon*. And, as the report stated, "Many of the students who refused to attempt problems because they *felt* they did not know the answer did, in reality, have sufficient information." What this means is that they had enough information to *reason through* to an answer. But a typical response among such low scorers is, "It's too hard," or "This doesn't make sense," or "It's very complicated." Such complaints are often evidence that a low scorer has given up before trying a problem that *could* have been solved.

Here are some of the basic principles in reasoning through.

Your frame of mind is important. Researchers note that high scorers and "testwise" students are prepared to tackle longer questions than are low scorers, and to spend more time on a question that is unclear. This readiness is partly the result of the fact that high scorers believe that questions *can* be reasoned through and are consistently more confident of their ability to solve problems than are low scorers.

Check the key terms to be sure you're focusing on the demands of the question. Earlier in this chapter was a list of some major key words and terms that might appear on short-answer questions. Underline or circle such key terms if you're permitted to mark the question paper.

One of the following is a cause of the other three. Which one is the cause?
(a) New York City is the country's major commercial center.
(b) New York City has excellent natural waterways and harbors.
(c) New York City has the country's largest population.
(d) New York City is a major shopping center.

The same caution holds true for essay questions. While teachers may not use operative words very precisely, professional test-makers often do. Words like *describe, illustrate, show, distinguish, compare, outline, review, trace, summarize,* and *list* ask you to do specific—and different—things. We'll deal with essay testing in greater detail in a later chapter.

Narrow your choices. In objective or short-answer tests, find the "distractors" that don't fit, the nonfunctional "filler" items, the choices that say the same things in different words, the mutually exclusive items. There will be a good deal on such analysis in the chapter on the classroom objective test.

Translate and substitute material. In mathematics, for example, you might try a "dry run," substituting smaller and simpler numbers for larger numbers or for symbols, in order to establish the principle involved or the appropriate formula. For example, you may have to find the circumference of a circle but, like many students, you can't remember whether the formula to use is $2\pi r$ or πr^2. Substitute the number 5 for r and calculate:

$$2\pi r = 10\pi \qquad\qquad \pi r^2 = 25\pi$$

You probably realize that the area of a circle is generally larger than its circumference, so $2\pi r$ is logically the formula for the circumference. Similarly, if a question asks you to find a percentage and you're not sure of the procedure, you might remember that the sales tax in your state is a *percentage* of the price of the item; how do you calculate the sales tax?

Using much the same kind of substitution, you can simplify language by replacing relatively unfamiliar words with more common synonyms in order to make sense of a sentence of a paragraph. Substituting an illustrative specific name or example for an abstract term can often help you to think through a problem. In the University of Chicago study, for example, some students had trouble answering a question that dealt with "corporate enterprise in America." As a result of questions by the experimenter, these students came to realize that the Ford Motor Company was an example of "corporate enterprise" and were able to deal with the question.

Break the question down into manageable parts. There was a fairly lengthy illustration of such a breakdown in Chapter 2 in the discussion of Whimbey's work with students. The idea of attacking a problem through such a breakdown is based on the principle that *you usually know more about a problem than you think you do.* Many test-takers become confused when faced with a long and complex task; but by separating it into smaller sections and dealing with one at a time, they can solve the problem.

Use the test itself as a source of information. You can often use information from one item to answer another. For example:

Which one of the following is a vertebrate animal?
(a) starfish   (b) stingray   (c) sea urchin   (d) grasshopper
(d) earthworm

Which one of the following is an invertebrate animal?
(a) shark   (b) lamprey eel   (c) crocodile   (d) starfish   (e) trout

If you know that a stingray is a *vertebrate,* you have just acquired some valuable information: that starfish, sea urchins, grasshoppers, and earthworms are *invertebrates.* Often several items on the test will deal with the same general area of information and, if you're alert, you may be able to cross-reference the information on them. This kind of application is easier to perform if you get into the habit of thinking of the test as a valuable surce of information.

Summary:
• Check the key terms.
• Narrow your choices through elimination.
• Translate and substitute terms to simplify a question.
• Break the question into manageable parts.
• Use whatever information you may gain from other items.

REVIEW YOUR ANSWERS

Following up on the matter of using your time intelligently, use whatever time you have at the end to review your answers. Everybody knows that moment of panic when you're about halfway through your test and Joe Whiz gets up, hands in his paper, and walks out. Joe may really be good at test-taking—or he may be a low scorer who rushed through, or he may be grandstanding to show how bright he is. Studies show that often the first people out of the room have just *failed.* Stay the full time; any time left over should be used to review your answers.

If you realize that your first response may be wrong, don't be afraid to change your answers. Bull-session wisdom tells you to leave an answer alone because your first impression is probably right; in this case, bull-session wisdom is not so wise. Studies at ETS and elsewhere show that more answers are changed from wrong to correct than from correct to wrong. But don't rely on anybody's statistics. If you change an answer, it should be done only because *you* really believe that your changed answer is correct.

HOW DO STUDENTS RANK PRINCIPLES OF TESTWISENESS?

In a number of studies of testwiseness among high school and college students, high-scoring test-takers were asked for the secrets of their success. Typical was the ranking of one group of 240 high school students asked by a

Cornell University investigator to offer suggestions to a new student who had just moved to their school and was unfamiliar with the tests that were given there. In the order of their ranking, here are their tips:

Read directions (or questions) carefully	44%
Don't spend too much time on one question	27%
Recheck your answers for errors	20%
Guess if you don't know the answers	18%
Eliminate possible foils and distractors	17%
Look for leads from other questions	13%
Answer easier questions first	8%
Plan your time	7%
Don't read into questions (or answers) too deeply	5%

A group of college students thought that the two most important reasons for their high performance on tests were "test understanding" and "comprehension and reasoning ability." Interestingly enough, knowledge of subject matter was *not* usually listed among the top reasons given in any of the studies in which students themselves were asked about test success.

5.
Handling the Classroom Objective Test

Of all the tests you'll be taking, the ordinary teacher-made classroom test is probably the most poorly designed. This can be both good and bad as far as you're concerned. The major advantage is that most such tests abound in clues and giveaways that can help you to beat the test. But a really bad test can be *so* bad that it's essentially a guessing game. There may not even be a logical basis for figuring out what the instructor had in mind from the question itself, even if—*especially* if—you know the subject. For example:

> Through a given point only one line can be drawn parallel to a given straight line   T   F

If your knowledge of geometry is limited to a dim recollection of some axioms and theorems, you'd have no trouble with this. But if you know too much, you've got a problem. Is the instructor testing you on your memory of Euclid's fifth postulate? Or on your knowledge of the fact that there are non-Euclidean geometries that reject this postulate?

In this case, you're left with two strategies. One is to circle T—and then add, to let the teacher know that *you* know "(if one accepts Euclid's axiom)." The other— and probably the more useful, because you'll have this kind of problem all through the term or semester or quarter—is to know the teacher or professor. Find out if he or she is a mousetrapper out to catch the unwary, or just a well-meaning but rather imprecise soul who sincerely wants to know if people grasp fundamental ideas and facts but has never really learned how to find out.

In any event, you should realize that it's to your advantage to have as many quizzes and tests as possible. Only in this way can you study the teacher.

The tests themselves can provide some quick answers. The chances are that the skim-through will indicate the kinds of answers the examiner has in mind and may help you with responses to specific questions. Here are some general rules for dealing with those classroom objective (or short answer) tests.

COMPLETION TESTS

Those fill-in-the-blank tests pose a real problem, in which you have to decide which of a multitude of fill-ins the teacher or prof had in mind when the item was written.

Abraham Lincoln was born in _____.

Kentucky? 1809? A wilderness cabin: Hodgenville? The backwoods? Just because your answer is correct and true and accurate, you can't assume that you'll get credit for it. For example, if you wrote "wedlock" in the space, you'd be perfectly right— but don't try it! Teachers can be notoriously touchy if they think you're being cute or funny. But many times you really can't tell what the instructor had in mind, and many teachers are defensive if their precision is questioned. Some teachers argue that some correct answers are "more" correct than other correct answers. Unfortunately, if you run into one of these, logic is not usually a compelling argument; the defensive teacher is usually defending his or her own prejudiced choice.

While there is no adequate mechanism for coping with a really bad completion test, there are some defense devices and strategies that should help you.

If you don't know an answer, guess. There are hardly ever penalties for guessing on a completion test. Write in an answer, even if your mind has gone as blank as the space on the paper. In guessing, try to be as *general* as the teacher will allow. For example:

The quotation, "He that is giddy thinks the world turns round" comes from _____.

If you've been studying Renaissance writers, Shakespeare could be a good bet, and you might just write "Shakespeare." If you know from experience that the teacher insists on more specific answers, you might reason from the tone of the quotation that it is more likely to have come from a comedy than from a tragedy, and you might try "one of Shakespeare's comedies." If this instructor demands exact answers, there's no way around it—stab at one of Shakespeare's comedies, if you can remember the names of any. (It was *Taming of the Shrew,* by the way.) If you think that it could be either *As You Like It* or *Taming of the Shrew,* write your first choice and then add the other as a possibility. You might get partial credit if one is correct.

Use grammatical clues. Obviously, the answer you choose should be grammatically consistent with the stem phrase or sentence. If the blank is preceded by *an,* you know that the answer begins with a vowel. Grammatical clues include tense; singular or plural forms of pronouns or verbs; and the use of modifiers, adverbs, and adjectives that can help you focus on the type of answer.

Use length and number of blanks. Obviously, the space should be long enough to write in the correct response, so the length of the space or the use of broken lines to indicate several words can be clues. (Experienced teachers, though, eliminate this clue by providing long single lines for all responses.)

For a variety of reasons, completion items are practically nonexistent on professionally prepared exams. They can't be machine-scored, they're susceptible to a variety of correct answers, and they are used principally to test for memory of specifics rather than for the application of broad principles. Fortunately, they've become increasingly rare nowadays even on teacher-made exams, largely because of the arguments that develop in a classroom over the possible correct answers.

Normally, only the least sophisticated (or laziest) teachers still give completion tests; they're easy to make up, because the instructor can simply copy out sentences from the textbook and leave out words and phrases. So when you study for such tests, hit the textbooks and your notes, and focus on key words and phrases.

TRUE–FALSE TESTS

If a true-false test is of the simple type, you just have to read a statement and mark it *true* or *false.* Your chances of guessing right are very good—if the test is short. The odds against guessing right might rise rapidly as the test gets longer.

Number of true-false items	Chance of getting a 70% by wild guessing
10	1 out of 6
25	1 out of 50
50	1 out of 350
100	1 out of 10,000
200	less than 1 out of 1 million

True-false questions are tough to handle, because they're so likely to be ambiguous. Few statements are absolutely and unqualifiably true *or* false. So the test-maker often presents statements that are only approximately true, or focuses on trivia and minutiae. In this kind of test, as in the completion test, you're likely to have trouble if you think beyond rote memorization or if you know too much. Here are questions that could be much more difficult if you think.

Light travels in a straight line.   T F

Everybody who reads the news knows that the disposal of nuclear wastes is a growing problem.   T F

Students who can't remember anything very complicated, and who get headaches from thinking, will have no trouble with these. But you know that there are all kinds of conditions that will bend or diffuse light waves. And you can't figure out if the second question is asking you to agree that the disposal of nuclear wastes is a growing problem, or that everybody who reads the news knows about the problem.

How do you handle such items? Defensive test-taking requires a knowledge of the basic objectives of the test-maker. Review the section in Chapter 4 on figuring out the test-maker's intent. Here are some general rules for true-false tests.

When in doubt, guess. There is rarely a penalty for guessing on such tests. And remember that the odds in short tests are very much in your favor.

Be alert to exceptions or false parts. Any false section makes the *whole* statement false. And the statement should be true without exception. If you're not sure what the instructor has in mind, qualify your statement in the margin with a comment explaining your answer. For example:

Plant growth depends on the interaction of water, carbon dioxide, and sunlight.   T Ⓕ

Not all plants contain chlorophyll or need sunlight for growth

Play the odds. There are usually more true than false items on most tests, probably because it is easier for a test-maker to write a true statement than to create a plausible false one.

Look for specific determiners. In a classic study of many classroom tests, Herbert E. Hawkes, E. F. Lindquist, and C. R. Mann pointed out:

Four out of five statements containing "all" were false;
Four out of five statements containing "none" were true;
Nine out of ten statements containing "only" were false;
Three out of four statements containing "generally" were true;
Four out of five "enumeration" statements were true;
Two out of three "reason" or "because" statements were false;
Three out of four statements containing "always" were false;
The longer the statement, the more likely it is to be true.

(Dr. Dell Lebo, who teaches test-taking techniques in Jacksonville, Florida, disagrees with the last point. Wrote Dr. Lebo, in response to an article of mine on test-taking: "It has been my experience that the longer a true-false question is, the greater are its chances of being false." Let me know *your* experiences.)

Watch for traps. If you find trap or catch questions, they are warnings to proceed with caution; a test-maker who thinks in terms of such questions is likely to have booby-trapped the whole test.

> The capital of New York State is not Albany.   T   F

Unless you read the question very carefully, you may miss the *not* buried in the statement—another reminder to read instructions and questions carefully. Here's another type:

> The Sherman Anti-Trust Act, passed in 1870, declared combinations in restraint of trade illegal.   T   F

The statement is false, because the Sherman Anti-Trust Act was passed in 1890 (remember the rule about false parts). But because the false section is hidden away in a subordinate clause, many students will focus on the major element, which is true.

Professional test-makers consider such traps cheap shots. As early as 1936, one book on test-making stated, "They tend to trip up the student whose knowledge is sound but who naturally ignores what should logically be minor or unimportant elements in the statement and who interprets a statement in the straightforward fashion characteristic of ordinary reading." Such traps rarely appear in professionally designed tests, but you'll find them often in tests made by teachers who confuse testing for knowledge or understanding with testing for mental alertness or testwiseness or suspicion.

Similar to the buried item is the composite, where the generally skimmed *first* section is false: For example:

> In Islamic art, only the representation of nonreligious human figures is permitted, because Moslems take literally the warning against making graven idols.   T   F

The second part of this statement (the *because* part) is true, and many students, including those who really know better, get caught. They assume that the *because* clause will contain the element to be judged true or false. Again, professionals rarely indulge in this kind of trap, but teachers often do. Remember: read all parts of a true-false statement, and if *any* part is false, the *whole* statement is false.

True-false tests are not as common as they used to be in professionally made tests because they tend to be ambiguous and they lend themselves to guessing. But you'll still find them in the classroom. A modified true-false test cuts down on the elements of ambiguity and guessing. If the statement is false, you will get credit only if you write in the correct word or phrase for the underlined or italicized term. For example:

> Water boils at 212 degrees *Centigrade*.   T   Ⓕ *Fahrenheit*

Here at least you know that you don't have to consider sea level or adulteration. If you draw a complete blank, circle T. You'll still have a 50-50 chance of getting it right.

MATCHING QUESTIONS

These exercises usually consist of two columns of items that have to be paired. One column may consist of names, words, terms, numbers, or principles. The other contains definitions, descriptions, computations, or applications.

If the test is going to consist largely of matching questions, study from your text or notes in terms of pairs or sets of words, that is, terms and phrases that are associated. Concentrate on connecting them.

Matching columns can be so long and the arrangement so complicated that you spend more time searching for the right answer than in figuring it out. When professionals compose matching exercises, they usually minimize waste time by organizing the data in some logical way, by alphabetizing names or putting dates in chronological order. Unfortunately, on most teacher-made tests, both columns are likely to be long and jumbled up. There are some general principles, though, that can help you cut down on waste time and confusion.

Work down one column at a time—the one with the longer items. The usual method of most test-takers is to read each item in the left-hand column and then to skim the list on the right to find the match. But if the shorter items (names, dates, etc.) are in the left-hand column, as they often are, you'll find yourself rereading the longer items many times. If you work down the column with the *more complex statements,* then you'll be rereading the shorter items, which can be read more quickly, kept in mind more easily, and compared more readily. As you find the matching item, draw a line through it or put a dot next to it so that you don't keep coming back to it over and over. This hint is useful only if you're taking the usual test in which you are instructed to use each item only once. On some matching tests, you can choose an item more than once. Be sure you know which kind you're working on. If the instructions are vague, ask the proctor or instructor.

Clarify the relationship between the columns. Normally, if one column contains names and the other identifications, or if one lists dates and the other presents events, the relationships are fairly obvious. But you could find one like the following, adapted from a publication by the New York State Bureau of Examinations and Testing.

Column A
_____ a. lens
_____ b. mercury
_____ c. transistor
_____ d. electromagnet
_____ e. filament

Column B
1. barometer
2. electric light bulb
3. gasoline engine
4. microscope
5. periscope
6. radio
7. telephone

As you glance down the lists, you should become aware of the organizational scheme and the relationship between the lists. In the columns above, you should have seen that column B contains instruments, machines, or devices, and that column A contains *parts* of such instruments or devices. It seems obvious, even in the absence of clear instructions, that you are being asked to find the device in column B in which the parts in column A are used.

Start with the items of which you're certain. On matching tests, if you make one mistake, you're likely to mess up a number of other pairs. You'll find, too, that as you reduce the number of pairs remaining, some of the more uncertain ones will seem more clear. After you've marked off the certain items, go over the remaining ones and apply the devices outlined in Chapter 4 on reasoning through to an answer.

Look for built-in clues. Professionals generally use only parallel or homogeneous columns—that is, if one column contains dates, it will contain *only* dates. But because teachers tend to jumble up such items as names, dates, laws, and terms, you can often reduce the actual choice to those items that obviously go with names or dates or laws. Below is a sample matching test in American History, adapted from an article by Harry Berg in the *35th Yearbook* of the National Council for the Social Studies. This test is full of logical and verbal clues, probably more than would appear in most classroom tests. See if you can find them.

Directions: Find the item in column B that best matches the name or date in column A. Use each item only once.

Column A
1. Virginia and Kentucky Resolutions
2. Napoleonic Decrees and Orders in Council
3. Tecumseh
4. Federalists
5. Hartford Convention
6. 1803
7. Impressment
8. Alien and Sedition Acts
9. Lewis and Clark
10. Genêt
11. Embargo Act
12. War Hawks
13. Alexander Hamilton

Column B
( ) a. French minister to the U.S.
( ) b. Meeting to protest War of 1812
( ) c. Seizure of American seamen
( ) d. Gave president power to deport aliens
( ) e. Declared nullification the proper remedy for unconstitutional acts
( ) f. French and English orders against neutral carrying trade
( ) g. Explorers of Louisiana Territory
( ) h. Prohibited American vessels from sailing to foreign ports
( ) i. Leader of Indian uprisings
( ) j. Those who demanded war with England
( ) k. Party opposed to Republicans
( ) l. Year in which Louisiana was purchased

Did you notice in:
   a. that only one name in column A seems French?
   b. that the word *convention* means *meeting?*
   c. that *impressment* means pressing into service—or *seizure?*
   d. that one item in column A has the word *alien* in it?
   e. that after eliminating all the items with verbal clues, only two items remain in column A, so you now have a 50-50 chance of getting this one by guessing?
   f. that the word *decree* means *order,* and that the same item in column A refers to the French leader Napoleon?
   g. that only one item in column A has plural names?
   h. that *emgargo* means *prohibit?*
   i. that there is only one name of an Indian in column A?
   j. that one item in column A matches this one by clear verbal association?
   k. that there is only one political party listed in column A?
   l. that there is only one year in column A?

MULTIPLE-CHOICE TESTS

Multiple-choice questions have become the standard type of mass examination items. Such items minimize the ambiguity that marks so many completion and true-false tests. In addition, multiple-choice tests have clear advantages for the commercial test market, the major one being that they can easily be scored by machine.

The multiple-choice form can be used to test at virtually every level of cognitive, or thinking, ability—except for creativity. A well-designed test can measure the abilities to understand, analyze, interpret, and apply learning. Like most other tests, however, the majority of multiple-choice tests are not very well designed. The best have been prepared by professionals for use in standardized testing, and even in this area the majority of tests are not very good. Teacher-made multiple-choice tests can be pretty awful. Not only do most of them focus on memorization (the lowest level of cognition), but they tend to be mechanically weak. Most such tests, in other words, are loaded with clues and road signs.

Because multiple-choice tests are rapidly becoming the most common of all objective test types, you should become familiar with their construction and ways of coping with them. A multiple-choice question has a *stem*—either an incomplete sentence or a direct question—followed by a number of options, usually four or five. Normally, only one of the options is correct. The others are known as *distractors,* and they are clearly incorrect, although test-makers try to make them as plausible as possible. Some questions may ask you to select *more* than one correct answer, so be alert to instructions. On some tests you may be asked to choose the "most correct" of several correct answers; this is a patently unfair and unreasonable demand, because you're being asked to make a value judgment about apparently objective data. For some peculiar reason, though, you may find this type even on some standardized tests.

One professionally designed question type involves a *combination* of correct answers; there may be a list of lettered options, and the answer choices may appear as groupings of options. For example:

Which of the following methods of improving plants or animal breeds are correctly paired with examples of applications?
(a) selection—racehorses   (b) grafting—seedless oranges
(c) hybridization—Kansas red wheat   (d) mutation breeding—silver foxes

The correct combination is   1. a, c, and d   2. b, c, and d   3. a, b, and c
4. all of these   5. none of these

It's much harder to use verbal or logical clues to find the correct choice in this kind of question. But it's also much more difficult for the test-maker to make up a combination question than to produce a straight multiple-choice question.As a result, you probably won't see too many combination questions on classroom tests.

Some general advice, first, on studying for multiple-choice tests and on test-taking strategy. Rely first on the general strategies for taking tests outlined in Chapter 4 and on reasoning techniques. Use flaws in test construction as a last resort. For one thing, the clues and giveaways may not always be there when you need them. Study for such tests by concentrating on *sets* of words, phrases, and ideas rather than on isolated bits of information. Look for the connections that tie the items together.

Rely first on reasoning strategies
Review the general strategies in Chapter 4. The major ones:
Skim the test to get an overview of intent and M.O.
Read instructions carefully; understand what is wanted.
Answer what is asked, not what you *think* should be asked.
Read the questions carefully; don't jump to conclusions.
Focus on key words and terms; underline them if permitted.
Narrow choices through elimination.
Translate and substitute terms to simplify a question.
Break the question into manageable parts.
Use whatever information you can get from other items.

Keep the focus of the question in mind. This is an aspect of reading the question carefully. For example:

The Polish astronomer Copernicus questioned the common belief that   (a) the earth is the center of the universe   (b) the planets revolve around the sun (c) the planets move in elliptical orbits   (d) the planets are extremely hot

As you run down this list of options, you would probably notice that only (b) and (c) are true. Low scorers would tend to choose one of these as the answer. But the question doesn't ask you to choose a *true* statement; it asks you to pick the one that Copernicus *questioned,* which would be (a). Reminder: circle the key word or term.

Ignore the "window dressing." Get immediately to the heart of the question and ignore distracting nonfunctional matter.

> *It is generally accepted today as a principle of health maintenance that proper diet is important for a healthy individual to resist disease. Which illness is prevented by including citrus fruit in the diet?* (a) pellagra (b) scurvy (c) rickets (d) diabetes (e) all of these

You should quickly have realized that the first sentence of the question is window dressing and concentrated on the question itself.

Use logic where possible. Many test items call for an application of common sense, rather than specific learned knowledge. For example:

> *Which one of the following would be the most reliable source for accurate information on the storming of the Bastille in Paris on July 14, 1789?*
> (a) An account in a revolutionary circular, July 21, 1789
> (b) An historical novel about the French Revolution
> (c) An account in an English newspaper on July 17, 1789
> (d) A description of the events in the diary of an eyewitness

You don't have to know much about the French Revolution to figure out that the most accurate account would probably be the one written in a private diary by an eyewitness.

Sometimes just one small item of information is all you need to turn the question into a common-sense one. Here is an example from the famous New York State Regents Examination in American History and World Backgrounds.

> *William Gladstone said in 1864. "They who in quarrels will interpose, will often wipe a bloody nose." This statement made during the U.S. Civil War might have been prompted by the* (a) issuance of the Emancipation Proclamation by President Lincoln (b) plan of radicals for reconstruction of the South (c) visit of Russia's fleet to Northern ports (d) proposal that Great Britain support the South.

If you know that Gladstone was a British prime minister, or even if you just have a vague recollection of having heard the name in connection with Britain, the answer is obviously (d)—unless the test is deliberately loaded with options that are false as well as incorrect. Even if you're at a complete loss, logic should tell you that neither Lincoln nor the radicals were "interposing," or interfering, in the affairs of the Americans.

Here is another type of question in which knowledge of *part* of an answer provides the essential clue.

> *Which of the following American cities is in the Southeast?*
> (a) Atlanta (b) Charleston (c) Jacksonville (d) none of these (e) all of these

If you recognize that Atlanta and Charleston are in the Southeast, you would choose (e), even if you had never heard of Jacksonville.

Try working backward from the answer. This is a useful way of handling a problem on a trial-and-error basis when you know some of the peripheral data but can't recall a formula or technique. It's often used in math questions.

Which number is the largest prime factor of 87?
(a) 11   (b) 3   (c) 7   (d) 29

In dealing with a question like this, you would start by dividing 87 by the largest number presented to see if it fits. Professionals, and some experienced teachers, sometimes block this test-taking device by leaving out the correct answer and substituting *none of these.* But most teachers either overlook the possibility of working backwards, or don't really care how you get the answer.

Look for clues and giveaways

It's tempting to look for the flaws and test weaknesses first. Somehow it suggests that you're getting something for nothing, and often you *do* get dividends on testwiseness of this sort. But there is a caution that should be pointed out: use flaws and test weaknesses only as a last resort.

This caution has nothing to do with honesty or some misguided sense of ethics. You're penalized enough by instructors who don't know how to test for what you know or understand, so anything you get from utilizing poor test construction is only a balancing device. The reason you should save such strategies for last is that they may be undependable if your instructor is experienced or as testwise as you. (Remember, even your faltering old teacher was a test-taker once, and he or she might just have learned something from the experience.) But, by and large, most teacher-made tests are badly flawed and you should be able to pick up some credits. Here are some of the major clues.

Look for specific determiners. As in true-false questions, such terms as *all, none, always,* and *never* seldom appear in correct options. If you *do* find that such words seem to be appearing in options that you know or figured out are correct, be warned! The test-maker may deliberately be using such terms in correct items to trap those who rely heavily on test flaws. Also, you should be aware that some instructors—fortunately a minority—use such terms with really amazing imprecision. (" 'When *I* use a word,' Humpty Dumpty said rather scornfully to Alice, in *Through the Looking Glass,* 'it means just what I choose it to mean—neither more nor less.' ") One professor of criminal justice at the University of Florida tells his classes *after* a test that when he uses the word *always* on an exam question, it means "most of the time."

Look for stereotyped phrasing. Often the stem and the correct response are taken directly from the textbook or a lecture. So look for familiar wording in combination. But be careful of booby traps, like slipping into a stereotyped phrase the word "not," which would change its meaning drastically.

Look for verbal clues. The examples presented in the matching exercise earlier in this chapter would apply here as well. (Matching tests are really variations on the multiple-choice format.) Some verbal clues:

- Is there a repetition in the stem and one of the options of the same word or a synonym? For example:

The commission that controls railroad shipping between the states is   (a) the Federal Trade Commission   (b) the National Chamber of Commerce   (c) the Interstate Commerce Commission   (d) the Better Business Bureau

This one might seem tougher than it really is, because there are two options with the word *commission,* and one of them also has the word *trade.* But option (c) is the best bet because it contains all three elements: interstate, commerce, and commission.

- Can you find common verbal associations? For example:

Which president warned, in his farewell address, against involvement in entangling foreign alliances?
(a) Washington   (b) Jackson   (c) Monroe   (d) Truman

You have probably heard of "Washington's Farewell Address," even if you haven't the foggiest notion of what Washington said in it. All you have to do, in a question like this, is identify the elements of common verbal associations—words that go together—like *Monroe-and-Doctrine,* or *stimulus-and-response.*

- Can you find in one of the responses an implied definition of a key word in the stem? For example:

An industry that is vertically organized   (a) controls distribution and ultimate purchase   (b) controls the production of similar items   (c) is nonunion   (d) owns all the means of production upwards from mine to factory

Even if the words *upwards* were absent from (d), the testwise student should be aware of the implied definition of the term *vertically organized* in option (d).

Look for uniformities in the placement of correct answers. Because teachers are likely to think first of the correct choice, many consistently place correct choices at or near the beginning of a group. Others may overcompensate by placing them at or near the end, and still others may tend to cluster them in the center. Some, to make scoring easy, set up an easy-to-mark pattern, such as CADB. As you proceed, be alert to possible patterns.

Check for grammatical consistency between the stem and the correct response. Some teachers are careless about maintaining such grammatical consistency in the distractors, or incorrect options. A stem that calls for a plural noun, for example, may be followed by several incorrect responses with singular nouns. You should be aware, though, that some teachers deliberately mislead by *knowingly* using the wrong connector, such as *an* where *a* would be appropriate. While such instructors think they're trapping the guesser, the effect is likely to be that those who *know* the answer are confused and choose an incorrect option.

Recognize rankings and orderings. In questions involving dates or quantities, there is usually a spread on either side of a correct response. One item is likely to be too low and one too high. In such rankings, the correct choice is usually one of the middle items—in size or chronology, not in position. For example:

The speed of light is approximately   (a) 50,000 miles a second   (b) 250,000 miles a second   (c) 122,500 miles a second   (d) 186,000 miles a second

The testwise student who doesn't have the answer at hand will eliminate choices (a) and (b) and then guess between the two middle options, (c) and (d).

Look for overlong or unusually short items. To avoid ambiguities, the test-maker may have been exceptionally precise in phrasing the correct option. Less frequently, some test-makers load down incorrect responses with erroneous and misleading qualifiers, so that they are longer than the correct choice. You'll see very quickly if there is a pattern of long or short correct answers.

Look for implausible choices. For example:

Cytoplasm is   (a) the dense center of a cell   (b) a type of building
(c) a covering of a cell   (d) the main bulk of a cell

Even if you don't know much about biology, and never heard of cytoplasm, it should be pretty obvious that (b) does not belong in the list, especially since all the other choices deal with cells.

Remember that you can lose points on a completion item by being cute or funny. Well, teachers sometimes give away points because they can't resist including flippant or humorous choices for the sake of chuckles.

If a newborn infant's hands are placed over a broom handle, the infant will   (a) cry
(b) wave the broom   (c) grasp the broom handle tightly   (d) sweep the floor

Choices (b) and (d) are so farfetched that any normally bright student will eliminate them immediately. Sometimes a teacher may be willing to give away a choice or two for the sake of audience appreciation (a lot of teachers see themselves as actors). But regardless of intent, take advantage of the free ride. Such giveaways, intentional or otherwise, are common on teacher-made tests. Hunt and Metcalf, the authors of a well-known book on teaching, write, "Occasionally a multiple-choice item is so constructed that all but the correct choice seems implausible. Such an item measures nothing except the ability of a student to read." That's not entirely true; low scorers often overlook even such giveaways because they've already given up on the test and work on the know/don't know principle.

Look for the generalized response. Often the correct choice will be more general in nature than the incorrect choices so that it has a broader applicability.

Look for the qualified response, modified to make it more precise. Choices containing such words as *generally, often,* or *seldom* frequently are correct responses.

Look for the two items that cover the field. In many multiple-choice tests, two items may contradict each other, and may both be wrong. But if the contradictory items cover all possibilities, then the correct choice must be one of them.

Which one of the following statements is true?
(a) Bacteria cannot develop from lifeless matter
(b) Bacteria can reproduce only through binary fission
(c) Bacteria can develop through spontaneous generation
(d) Bacteria reproduce sexually.

You should have noticed that (a) and (c) contradict each other. But more than this, they cover all possibilities between them: if one is incorrect, the other *must* be correct. either bacteria *can* develop from lifeless matter (through spontaneous generation), or they can't. So, in effect, you have a two-choice question.

Look for overlapping items in which one choice automatically includes another. For example:

> *What percentage of Americans today live in cities?* (a) less than 30% (b) less than 50% (c) more than 50% (d) more than 80%

This question, taken from an actual classroom test, has *two* sets of logical giveaways. If (a) is true, then (b) *must* be true; and if (d) is true, then (c) must be true also. So the choice must be between (b) and (c). Moreover, these two items cover the field—see the last hint. If one is false, the other *must* be true. In spite of this double set of giveaways, it may be hard for you to believe that almost 10% of the class taking this test got the item wrong.

Look for overly technical language. Unless the instructor is out for blood, you won't be expected to know terms that hadn't been presented to the class either in the text or in lectures.

Look for emotionally charged words. You'll rarely find words like *foolhardy, stupid, nonsensical, ridiculous,* or *lunatic* in a correct response.

All the hints in this chapter are based on the assumption that you'll be taking a normally bad classroom test. But if a test is *really* awful, you may be stymied. The questions can be so bad that there is no way of ascertaining either the point of the question or the intent of the test-maker. For example:

> *Most nosebleeds* (a) occur in the anterior [front] portion of the nose (b) can be controlled by pinching the nostrils (c) require the insertion of a posterior pack (d) are the result of blows, nosepicking, or hard noseblowing.

This question involves no fewer than three separate and unrelated problems: the cause of nosebleed, the location of nosebleed, and the treatment of nosebleed—all in four choices. If you're looking for a single problem with one correct choice (which you have every right to find), you're in real trouble. Choices (a), (b), and (d) are all true, but they deal with different problems. What did the teacher have in mind as the central problem? And which is the "correct" answer?

In a case like this, your choice has to be pure guesswork. But write in the margin your *reason* for the choice, and take it up with the instructor afterwards. (Don't make an issue of bad questions during the test, beyond asking the proctor or instructor for clarification.) Test-makers, being human, will occasionally present bad or unanswerable questions. If you raise the issue diplomatically after the test, you should be able to convince the teacher that such questions should not be considered in calculating grades. If you have a really rigid and defensive teacher, you'll have to decide if the possible difference in test grade is worth antagonizing him or her.

6.
The Standardized Tests

Standardized testing has grown to such proportions that it's hard to find a profession or career in America today whose entrance is not guarded by standardized tests. "We're viewed as the nation's gatekeeper," admitted ETS president William Turnbull in 1978. If you want to get into college or become a lawyer, podiatrist, optometrist, real estate salesman, or plumber, chances are you'll have to pass a standardized test—often just to qualify for the training program!

The standardized test industry began around the turn of the century, shortly after Alfred Binet developed his idea of "standard tasks." The increasing numbers of college applicants made the old system of reviewing personal recommendations from teachers and other adults an awkward and obsolete way of screening would-be students. One of the innovations that developed, in large part to help screen college applicants, was the notion of school grades. (They haven't always been a part of the educational scene; the tradition of grades is a pretty new-fangled one.) About the same time, the College Board designed a standard entrance test for a few eastern colleges and universities. In 1926 the Board experimented with a new test, the SAT, which had been designed by Carl C. Brigham, a Princeton University psychologist. (Brigham, by the way, had a tendency to confuse numbers and values. It was he who, on the basis of scores on the army intelligence tests, concluded that whites from northern Europe were the most intelligent humans, and blacks the least intelligent. He warned that continued immigration from southern and eastern Europe would lower the average intelligence of Americans.) The Educational Testing Service, organized to administer the SAT, is now the giant of the testing industry, and the SAT itself probably the most widely used standardized test in human history. Located on 400 acres of rolling hills just outside Princeton, New Jersey, this $70 million-a-year enterprise now produces and administers scores of standardized tests for schools, businesses, and government agencies.

The phenomenal growth of ETS has developed only in the last few decades. In the 1951–1952 school year, only 81,000 SAT exams were given; by 1970, the figure was over 1.5 million. Most of the growth of the company (and the entire industry) is the result of the post-World War II baby boom and the increasing competition for a limited number of places in colleges, graduate schools, and professional schools.

The standardized test now follows graduates out of school into the professions and the trades. There are standardized certification and licensure exams for career fields ranging from social work and urban planning to firemen and U.S. Foreign Service officers. ETS even administers a test to applicants for the CIA!

Americans, who love to quantify information, are the most tested people who have ever lived. But the tremendous influence of the testers (and ETS, remember, is only one of the test publishers, although it's the biggest) has whipped up a stormy debate over the impact of the industry on our lives. Some professional groups, such as the National Education Association, have called for a moratorium on standardized testing pending a study of the effects of mass testing; a Harvard medical school professor has advocated boycotting the SAT; and Representative Michael Harrington of Massachusetts introduced a bill into Congress "to open the secrets of standardized testing to full public review."

But despite the growing concerns and the criticism, the use of standardized tests in this country is growing. Unless a better way is developed to decide who gets in and who gets what, say school and government officials, the test programs will be used to make the hard decisions and relieve the "decision makers" of the tough choices in weighing variables. (One has to wonder about the basic rationale, now that the use of standardized tests has spread to ascertain "readiness" for kindergarten.)

The debate has spurred the production of a mass of conflicting literature on the subject. The pamphlets pouring out of the test publishers' promotional offices invariably stress the benefits of tests to students and teachers alike. Students learn their hitherto hidden strengths and weaknesses, and teachers are provided the instruments with which to judge their students' abilities objectively and scientifically. In his book *The Schools,* Martin Mayer observes skeptically:

> *The purpose of the tests is not to judge either teachers' or children's work—God forbid—but to give that "guidance" which everybody needs if he or she is to live "a rich*

ongoing life. "*So runs the sales talk. Nevertheless, every observer of the schools has noted that it is the administrators, not the teachers or children, who are enthusiastic about these tests. Indeed, the Educational Testing Service, a nonprofit group which runs the most high-pressure test-selling operation in the country, has found it necessary in its literature to proclaim that "If a teacher is unsympathetic to a testing program . . . she is abdicating her rightful position."*

The critics point not only to the large number of really bad tests on the market (fortunately, the most widely used tests are well-designed, even if they don't always accomplish what the test givers hope), but to the misuse of even the best tests. The more reliable test publishers are sensitive to the obvious misuse of tests by faithful worshippers at the shrine of Scientific Objectivity, and blame the test buyers. After all, as Arthur E. Smith, Director of Educational Services of the National Merit Scholarship Corporation, argues, "the future of educational measurement is . . . in the hands of test-users—guidance directors, administrators, counselors, teachers and psychologists." Says one publishing official, "There are too many school administrators and counselors and admissions officers who look at test scores uncritically and ignore other variables; they tell kids and parents all kinds of nonsense with absolute assurance. That's like using powerful medicines without reading the label. But you can't just stop using medicine because some people misuse it." Many critics disagree, arguing that the industry doesn't try very hard to police its own ranks or to prevent misuse of its products. And since the 1960's, blacks have charged that the tests are culturally biased against minority groups, a charge vigorously disputed by the test publishers. ETS president, William Turnbull, argues that the scores merely reflect the educational disadvantages of minority students. (Since the black demonstrations of the mid-1960's, ETS has been careful to include excerpts from the works of black authors in its reading-comprehension tests.)

But, good or bad, used properly or not, there are likely to be at least one or two tests looming large in your future school or career choices. By and large, standardized tests are given for three professed purposes.

• Some are *diagnostic*; that is, they are supposed to pinpoint areas in which you need help.

• Some measure your *achievement* in a subject area. They are supposed to show how much you know or how well you can perform specified tasks. They may be used to decide whether you'll get a diploma, or whether your teacher will get a raise, or whether the school district will get federal funds, or whether the superintendent of schools will keep his job.

• Some are *predictive*. They claim to measure your aptitude for schoolwork or auto mechanics or card punch operation. They are used to prophesy how well you'll perform in school or on the job.

Let's examine some of these functions briefly and consider some of the questions that you might have about the tests.

DIAGNOSTIC TESTS

There are really two reasons for diagnosing your strengths and weaknesses. One is to determine where you should be placed, that is, to decide in what grade or class or track or program you belong. The other is to pinpoint the reasons for any problems you may have in reading or math or whatever, so that you can be given remedial treatment. Schools often claim that putting students in slow classes is in itself a remedial step, a claim that doesn't seem to be supported by most of the studies of tracking.

Achievement tests can be used for diagnosis, of course, but they'll tell you very little except that you're doing better than average or worse than average in certain areas. The problem is that a lot of teachers and schools are satisfied they've "diagnosed" your problem just by telling you that you're not doing as well as you should. Chances are that you've already figured that out and that you'd like to know specific weaknesses and what you should do about them.

The test-making art is well enough advanced so that tests *can* be used to pinpoint problems and causes for problems. Such tests are usually criterion-referenced tests; they are designed to find if you can perform specific tasks, not if you do as well as somebody else. Many tests that are called "diagnostic" are *norm-referenced* tests; they tell you how well you compare with the average person of your age, grade, or rank, usually reporting out in "profiles" or charts that show your rank in each category. If they are reported out in carefully planned subscores, even such norm-referenced tests can be useful in pointing to the general area in which you may have a problem. A good diagnostic test, though, must do more than just compare you with others; it must pinpoint your strengths and weaknesses and provide some direction for further instruction. Most norm-referenced tests don't do this.

Most so-called diagnostic tests are focused on reading and arithmetic, and most of them at very elementary levels. It's almost funny to see how many of the test-makers have confused their own narrow views for "reading ability." For example, on one "diagnostic" reading test, with impressive numbers of subtests, we get questions like this: a reading subtest ("Reading to Appreciate General Significance") presents to children a passage about Sally and Betty, who went to the circus, had a great time, and consumed fantastic quantities of popcorn, hot dogs, and pink lemonade "as if it were their last chance to enjoy these delicious treats." The test-takers are then asked to draw a line under the word that best describes how Betty and Sally felt at the circus: bored   excited   indifferent   ill   pained.

Now the student with imagination can figure out that after having gobbled all that garbage at the circus, either "ill" or "pained" would be pretty good descriptions of how these two would feel. But this imaginative kid would be marked wrong and considered less able to read "to appreciate general significance" than the dullard who wrote that they were "excited."

Still, a good diagnostic test is probably the most useful kind of test you can take. Some colleges, especially those with open admissions policies, have developed their own diagnostic tests. Some are pretty good; many are pretty bad. The use of a diagnostic test is great if the school has programs to help you *do* something about your problems.

ACHIEVEMENT TESTS

Most of the tests are *summative*: they describe what you have learned and how much you have learned. Such tests are used for a wide range of purposes, from measuring the effectiveness of a program in a school or a district to deciding whether you qualify for a job or a program. In some states they are used to determine whether you'll get a diploma.

Standardized tests are used to measure achievement in specified areas, either in general education or in specialized fields. Contrary to popular opinion, standardized test questions don't *have* to focus on rote memory, but most of the tests on the market do. Thumbing through the reviews in Buros' *Mental Measurements Yearbook* can be pretty depressing when you realize how much garbage is bought by schools each year to make critical and often irreversible decisions about students' personal worth and their futures. "The purpose of evaluation, as it is most frequently used in the existing education systems," write Benjamin Bloom and his colleagues in the *Handbook on Formative and Summative Evaluation of Student Learning,* "is primarily the grading and classifying of students.... As testing and other forms of evaluation are commonly used in the schools, they contribute little to the improvement of teaching and learning, and they rarely serve to ensure that all (or almost all) learn what the school system regards as the important tasks and goals of the education process."

PREDICTIVE TESTS: HOW WELL DO THEY PREDICT?

When we talk of predicting success, we're talking about mathematical odds. And some of the better tests on the market can predict *school* success. (By and large, test scores as predictors of success *on the job* have received failing grades in most of the studies.) But this success is limited to large groups of test-takers; the tests aren't nearly as useful in predicting for an individual. Furthermore, they don't predict nearly as well as many high school counselors think. Quite a few counselors think that the reassuringly high "coefficients of predictive validity" mean *odds.* They don't. For example, the overall coefficient of predictive validity of the SAT, possibly the best-designed standardized test in the world, hovers around .50 for all categories. But this doesn't mean that the prediction is 50% better than chance alone.

J. P. Guilford, an eminent psychometrician, uses a formula for an "index of forecasting efficiency." It's $E = 100 (1 - \sqrt{1 - r^2})$, where r is the coefficient of predictive validity. In his classic work, *Psychometric Methods,* Guilford concluded

73

that "Tests with a coefficient of validity less than .50 are practically useless, except in distinguishing between extreme cases, since at that value of *r* the forecasting efficiency is only 13.4 per cent."

Below is an "expectancy table" adapted from The Psychological Corporation's *Test Service Bulletin #45*. The figures are based on a coefficient of predictive validity of .50 and a success ratio of 50% (meaning that 50% of those who took the test will succeed in college, and 50% will fail).

Student's standing on the test in percentiles	Percentage of students who will succeed in each group	Odds of success for the individual in each group	
		based on pure chance	based on test rank
90–99	84	1 to 1	5 to 1
80–89	73	1 to 1	3 to 1
70–79	65	1 to 1	2 to 1
60–69	59	1 to 1	1 to 1
50–59	53	1 to 1	1 to 1
40–49	47	1 to 1	1 to 1
30–39	41	1 to 1	1 to 1
20–29	35	1 to 1	1 to 2
10–19	28	1 to 1	1 to 3
1–9	16	1 to 1	1 to 5

The fact is that even with Guilford's 13.4%, the odds based on test scores are better than the odds based on chance alone, *for those who score very high or very low.* As *Bulletin #45* points out, "A test of moderate validity can be efficient in quickly screening out the 'clearly ineligible' from the 'clearly eligible.'" But even this "efficiency" would be of little consolation to the one individual out of five in the very *lowest* group who is kept out of a program in which he *could* have done better than one out of five in the very *highest* scoring group. Remember that these odds are the house odds. That is, the colleges are covering themselves by trying to accept only those who are *most* likely to succeed. Those colleges that set cut-off scores are using odds based *only* on these tests (fewer undergraduate programs still set such scores than did in the past, but a good many graduate and professional schools do).

Banesh Hoffman, a mathematics professor at Queens College, is an outspoken critic of standardized tests in general. He is skeptical of claims that College Boards generally predict success in college, pointing out that the relationship between height and weight is also about .50. "Suppose you wanted to form a basketball team," he told an interviewer for *The National Elementary Principal* in 1975, "and you didn't know the heights of the players, so you picked them by their weight. You wouldn't get much of a basketball team. Several members would be

74

roly-poly. If that's the way you want to do education, I say that you're quite welcome to it."

Interestingly enough, high school grades are a better predictor of college grade point averages than are test scores; even the test-makers admit this. They argue, though, that using both high school grades and test scores is better than using either one alone. But a lot of colleges use "cutting scores" on the SAT and the ACT (American College Testing Assessment). That means that if you get below a certain score, many admissions officers won't even look at your high school grades. (I did a good deal of letter-writing and telephoning, but I couldn't find any colleges that set cut-offs based on high school grades. If there are any, I'd like to hear about them.)

Moreover, there is evidence that some nontest approaches actually predict better than test scores. In a 1976 study, Lila Norris and Warren Chapman compared tests and self-reports for students in ten community college courses; they reported that "For five of the courses the non-test validities were as high as or higher than the test validities, and in the other five the differences were modest."

Even though high school grades are the best single predictor for success in college, they are still not good predictors. Neither grades nor test scores describe the applicant in terms of interest, motivation, maturity, physical or emotional problems, personality factors, and the thousand-and-one other variables that account for success or failure.

The whole question of prediction is further complicated by the fact that the tests used to predict success in college are usually divided between verbal measurements and math measurements. These are two very different kinds of abilities and the tests are quite different in their prediction efficiency. For example, the SAT-V (verbal) is a far better predictor of success in college than is the SAT-M (mathematics), probably because almost all of college work is highly verbal while only a relatively small group of college students works with math. The math score, as a result, is really useful for only a small minority of students, normally those in some of the sciences, engineering, and accounting. But many college admissions officers insist on considering only the combined scores since many students don't know what their major will be. It's hard to see how someone who's good at verbal skills and poor at math will masochistically persist in engineering; and for graduate school applicants, this use of combined scores defies logic.

A number of professionals in testing and admissions have started to wonder if the tests are worth using. Writing in *Educational and Psychological Measurement,* Marvin Siegelman of New York's City College concluded from a study of CCNY students who had completed four years of study that "For males, the use of the SAT-V plus SAT-M with HSA [high school average] actually lowered the validity coefficients . . . from the predictions made from the HSA alone. . . ." The University of Wisconsin no longer requires the SAT; admissions director Lee Wilcox found that the scores were not particularly useful and were being ignored in many cases. And highly respected Bowdoin College in Maine has stopped demanding SAT scores for admission on the ground that their worth as a measure of true intellectual ability is questionable.

But most colleges still put a good deal of faith in the SAT, although most college applicants will find *some* college that will accept them regardless of score. The more prestigious schools do want high scores. Some college officials point to situations where a high SAT score persuaded them to take a chance on a student whose high school grades alone would have created strong doubts. On the other hand, the scores are more often used *against* candidates with good grades. "Take a kid from East Overshoe, Montana," the dean of admissions at Claremont College, California, told writer Diane Ravitch. "He has terrific grades, top of his class, wonderful recommendation from his principal; but his board scores are in the low 300's. The chances are very great that he will be over his head in our college." Well, maybe.

Remember, though, that college officials use the word "chances" when they deal for the house—and they want the house edge. Despite talk of social responsibilities, officials try to restrict acceptance to those who will "fit in" with their standards, not only academic, but social and philosophical as well. In 1961 the College Entrance Examination Board began publishing a *College Characteristics Handbook,* giving freshman class characteristics for a number of major colleges and universities. The purpose, presumably, was to promote the standardization (some call it the homogenization) of these schools by attracting to them new applicants similar to those students who were already there. Playing these odds strikes some as undemocratic because they close off opportunities for those who *might* make it but aren't permitted to try. Moreover, some critics argue, closing doors may serve the colleges' financial interests, but may not serve the interests of society. Describing the position of such critics, Joshua A. Fishman and Paul I. Clifford write, "The college experience itself is considered the best method of deciding who is and who is not fit to complete collegiate studies. A corollary of this view is that society and the individual are often more enriched by an academically unsuccessful stay of one year at the state university than by exclusion to begin with."

It is probably this kind of thinking that compelled a federal judge, in January 1978, to strike down barriers that kept some high school students from trying out for the football team. He wrote:

> *It may well be that there is a student today in an Ohio high school who lacks only the proper coaching and training to become the greatest quarterback in professional football history. Of course, the odds are astronomical against her. But isn't she entitled to a fair chance to try?*

The GRE (Graduate Record Examination) isn't even in the same league as the SAT; in fact, it's a notoriously bad predictor. Yet despite the fact that grades are a much better predictor, graduate school officials continue to place more weight on GRE scores than they do on college grades—even when the grades are from the same university and the same department! There are cases in which candidates for matriculation have been denied admission on the basis of GRE scores even when they have displayed straight A averages in prematriculation graduate work—exactly the kind of work that the GRE was designed to anticipate.

Use of the GRE is essentially an act of faith. College officials argue that the GRE's failure to predict is based on "restrictive validity"—that is, since only high scorers are admitted, there is no way of knowing how well the low scorers would have made out. Robyn M. Dawes, professor of psychology at the University of Oregon, wrote in *Science,* in February 1975, that "Studies involving admission variables will yield low correlations of necessity, and hence these low correlations cannot be used to determine whether the admission variables are any good. They may be. Or, on the other hand, they may be unfair or invalid—and their use may merely perpetuate an unfortunate status quo."

But whether or not the tests are good predictors, lots of people out there *think* they are. And that's what matters. No matter what you think of tests, good test scores provide more choices for you.

CAN COACHING RAISE YOUR SCORE?

The answer depends on whether we're talking about a narrow subject achievement test or one of the general "aptitude" tests such as the SAT or the ACT or the GRE.

For either type of test, coaching will help if you're new to the game. If you're not familiar with the format of standardized tests, then exposure to the tests alone will help you. (It's quite surprising how many test-takers lose credits because they haven't been taught the specifics of filling in the spaces in the mechanically scored answer sheets or taught to avoid stray pencil marks that may be picked up as wrong answers.) In addition, coaching can be quite useful if you're dealing with a specific subject; in this case it acts as a review. Keep in mind that the math sections of many aptitude tests *are* focused on specific subject matter. If you've been away from math for a while, coaching can definitely help, as can self-study.

In general, the test publishers claim that coaching won't help. A standard passage in the familiarization literature tells candidates for the SAT that the test measures abilities that have been developed from childhood, so that coaching ("vocabulary drill, memorizing facts and the like") won't do much to change a student's scores. Time spent on general reading and school assignments, claims ETS, will prove as helpful in preparing for the SAT, and far more useful in preparing for college.

A strikingly similar statement is made in the *ACT Assessment Counselor's Handbook* about preparation for the ACT. Such statements are supported by studies conducted by the testing organizations themselves. Most of the ETS experimental coaching programs resulted in score increases, but so small that they were less than the standard error of the tests. A typical conclusion was reported by Drs. John W. French and Robert E. Dear:

> *What is known about commercial coaching schools suggests that coaching by them would be less effective than that done in connection with these studies. The conclusion*

seems to be that an eager College Board candidate should not spend money on special coaching for the SAT. He would probably gain at least as much by some review of mathematics on his own and by the reading of a few good books.

The Educational Testing Service itself does admit two exceptions to its claims that coaching will not help. Students who aren't familiar with the standardized tests "may benefit from exposure to the format and procedures," says the SAT pamphlet, which suggests that reading the pamphlet itself is sufficient for this purpose. And students who have been out of contact with math are advised that they "may benefit from brushing up on the kind of thinking they must do to work with mathematical concepts."

The fact is, the math and verbal sections of these tests are very different from each other in a number of ways. For one thing, the math sections are much more "coachable" than the verbal sections. A study by Drs. Franklin R. Evans and Lewis W. Pike of ETS concluded that each of three math "item formats" was "susceptible to the special instruction specifically directed toward it." The experimental coached group gained, on an average, nearly a full standard deviation on these items. (If you want to see how much that means, refer back to the normal curve of distribution in Chapter 3.)

No matter what the CEEB (College Entrance Examination Board) or the ACTP (American College Testing Program) choose to call their math sections, they are subject achievement tests, as much as is a test in French or physics, and grouping them with the verbal tests as part of a "scholastic aptitude" package can be very misleading. As we've already seen, the math tests aren't very good predictors for those who don't intend to major in math-related subjects, and some experts wonder whether the math sections belong in tests that claim to predict college success in general.

In any event, all the ETS studies take a narrow view of coaching. John Smith, an ETS spokesman, told a senior editor of *The American School Board Journal,* "We don't feel short-term, intensive coaching makes a hell of a lot of difference."

A lot of school administrators don't believe this. James Guines, associate superintendent for instruction in the public schools of Washington, D.C., says that he doesn't know what the tests really measure, and he doesn't especially care. "I think they're going to be around for a long time," he says. "There's probably a bigger lobby to protect tests than there is to protect handguns and rifles. Cultural bias and racism—all that is really beside the point. I'm trying to help black kids beat the testing game. And I know how to do it." Washington's schools have engaged in a major all-out campaign. Students are exposed to tests, coached in test-taking, offered assembly programs in which they are taught time utilization and checking scoring techniques; even drilled in the mechanics of filling in computer-graded answer sheets. District teachers and counselors are scheduled for workshops in preparing students for such tests as the SAT. English and math departments may suspend regular instruction several weeks before important standardized tests in order to deal with just logic and reasoning skills. Does such coaching pay off? Guines claims he *knows* it does, based on his experience raising scores of prospective black teachers on the National Teachers Examination (NTE).

But ETS is probably right in arguing that the really big gains are made with test-takers who were pretty unsophisticated to begin with and who hadn't had much exposure to the tests. (However, a study with such students by S. O. Roberts and Don Oppenheim in 1966 showed very disappointing results, probably because the coaching was extremely short-term.) ETS is also right in arguing that most coaching schools or university coaching courses on GRE preparation won't help very much. For one thing, most such courses fit the ETS definition of coaching as short-term "vocabulary drill, memorizing facts, or the like." For another, most such courses are based on exposure and concentrate on "teaching" you, instead of finding out how you *think* and correcting you. Those coaching experiments that have been based on individual or small-group monitored work, however, have been quite successful. The hints in Chapter 2 on raising your IQ are equally appropriate for raising your aptitude test scores.

SOME OF THE MAJOR STANDARDIZED TESTS

The Scholastic Aptitude Test (SAT)

The SAT is probably the best-known and most widely used test in the history of formal testing. It is the central element of the battery of tests produced by ETS (there are 15 subject achievement tests offered as options), known collectively as the Admissions Testing Program or the College Boards. The College Boards play a major role in deciding in which college you'll be allowed to enroll and what shape your future will take.

Although many young Americans may think that the Boards have been around forever, their widespread use is only a couple of decades old. In fact, the group against which the SAT was "standardized" was a collection of 10,654 candidates who took the test in April 1941. It was *their* mean score that determined the specific value of the 500 score usually thought of as the mean for all the college applicants who take the test. It isn't—in fact, the decline in mean scores among applicants in recent years has set off a storm of debate as experts try to pinpoint the causes.

The SAT is taken by hopeful college applicants on six Saturday mornings each year in thousands of test centers throughout the country. Each test-taker pays (as of 1978) $7.25 for the privilege of taking a test that may slam shut the gates to the college of his or her choice.

The SAT consists of a verbal section and a mathematical section. In 1975 the exam was shortened from 3 hours to 2½ hours to provide a half-hour for a test in "standard written English"—the grammatical and spelling forms that are generally accepted as standard in written communication. This new test is in multiple-choice form, like the other sections. While the ETS has advised colleges to use the English usage test for placement purposes rather than for admission, there is some evidence that numbers of college admissions officers *have*, in fact, been using the test for admissions.

Some facts and figures:

• Approximately one-third of those who take the test apply to retake it. For two-thirds of those who take the test a second time, scores rise on the average of 15 to 20 points; they go down for the other third.

• There are alternative forms of the SAT, and no question appears twice on an SAT within a period of 18 months.

• Questions are developed by a staff of about 60 professionals at a total cost of well over $50 million.

• The difficulty of questions is carefully considered by test developers to maintain a range from easy to hard. A question is considered easy if more than 70% of the test-takers can answer it. Each item on the SAT is supposed to be answered by at least 10% of the test-takers and not more than 90%.

• A proportion of the questions—about one in six—is not officially scored; these are pretest items for future alternative forms of the test.

• A test question is reviewed by a battery of experts who consider its validity, its difficulty level, and the importance of the concept for which it tests. A question goes through more than a hundred steps before it is accepted, and may take as long as two years or more to find its way onto a test.

• Your scores are sent to you, to your school, and to three colleges of your choice. You should be aware that the report automatically includes all your *previous* scores on the College Boards. If you are no longer in high school, only current scores will appear. Scores can be cancelled in two ways: by filling out a form before you leave the examination room, or by writing to ETS within several days of the time you take the test. If you aren't well on the day of the test, or have some reason to think you didn't do well, it might pay to cancel your scores.

The level of your SAT scores may contribute more to shaping your own concept of yourself than to keeping you out of college. While SAT scores may affect your acceptance by a particular college, most applicants can get into college somewhere. More than half of all colleges accept at least 80% of their applicants. About 10% take practically every candidate; however, a large proportion of these are state universities that may subsequently flunk out large numbers of freshmen.

• For at least a decade, ETS has been sensitive to public criticism of its testing program. It routinely advises high school guidance counselors that its scores are broad generalized determinations, that there is an element of testing error, and that it is to be considered as only one factor out of many that should enter into decisions about test-takers. But there is considerable evidence that ETS's advice is not as persuasive as is the computerized printout number that suggests an awesome degree of exactness.

The Graduate Record Examination (GRE)

The GRE is brought to you by ETS, the folks who produced the SAT. Dating back to 1939, the GRE has become the major screening test used to decide if you can get into the graduate school of your choice. There are two types of tests given: the basic aptitude test, with sections on verbal ability, math, and "analytical reasoning"; and a series of advanced achievement tests in specific subjects. For a fee of $8 you can take the aptitude test on any of six mornings in January, February, April, June, October, and December. For $9 you have the privilege of appearing in the afternoon to take an advanced subject test, which is required by some graduate departments. If you take the economy package, you can buy a whole day of test-taking for $15. Your score will be sent to you, to your college, and to any three graduate schools of your choice.

The GRE was standardized against a group of 2,095 college seniors tested in 1952, and the scoring was arranged so that, like most ETS tests, the mean is 500. But since different kinds of people take the GRE each year, this score doesn't really represent the average of the groups taking the test at any one time, or even in any one year. The percentile group is a more meaningful form of figuring out where you stand. But the percentile you find reported on your official printout doesn't show where you stand in relation to the group with whom you took the test; it's based on a three-year "rolling norm."

The verbal section consists of analogies, antonyms, sentence completion, and reading comprehension. The math section (quantitative reasoning) includes exercises to test your computational skills, your familiarity with the property of numbers, and your ability to read, translate, and interpret graphs and charts. The new analytical reasoning section is designed to measure your ability to recognize logical relationships (for example, between a hypothesis and supporting evidence, or between stated facts and suggested explanations); to judge the consistency of interrelated statements; to draw warranted conclusions from a series of statements; to draw inferences from given data (including nonverbal and non-numerical data); and to find relationships between categories or groups. Of all the sections, the math is the most closely related to specific subject matter skills and is therefore the most coachable. The analytical reasoning is the least related to specific formal training.

The tests themselves, like the SAT, "are constructed, evaluated, and periodically revised in a highly workmanlike manner," according to the *Mental Measurements Yearbook*. The reliability is high; it's .90 or above for most of the tests.

There's one major problem. There's no real evidence that the GRE *does* predict how well you'll do in graduate school. Psychometricians suggest several reasons for this low predictive validity. Most important is the idea of "restriction of range." Again, since most schools accept only high scorers, there's no evidence on how well low scorers might have done. Moreover, a lot of the high scorers who were admitted don't make out well. So reliance on the GRE is fundamentally an act of faith.

Because most admissions officers are aware of this problem, many of them use the GRE as only one factor to be considered, along with undergraduate grades, experience, and so on. But too many schools or departments won't even consider you if you score below a certain cut-off point. The usual justification for such reliance on the GRE scores is that grading practices vary from college to college. But some admissions officers carry their faith in the GRE to an extreme approaching religious fervor. Many applicants who have established straight-A averages as nonmatriculated graduate students have been denied admission in the same school in which they earned as many as half the credits for a graduate degree—because the test score proclaimed that they shouldn't have been able to do it!

If you are a high scorer, of course, you have little to worry about beyond a light brushing up in math. If you're not, you have two choices: embark on a sustained program to develop test-taking skills, or find a school that doesn't worship the GRE.

The American College Testing Assessment (ACT)

The American College Testing Program of Iowa City is a young and aggressive rival of ETS. Since its founding in 1959, it has administered its ACT Assessment to a rapidly increasing number of students; the number had expanded to nearly a million in 1969–1970, but has slacked off slightly. More than 2,600 colleges and universities accept the results of the ACT Assessment, similar in nature to the SAT; many colleges will accept either SAT *or* ACT scores.

The ACTP makes the point that the examination itself is just the heart of an "assessment" that includes information to help you (and colleges) make decisions about your future; the information consists of your past experiences, abilities, interests, and goals. These facts are supplied by you on forms that can be computerized, then they are organized and reported out in a Student Profile Report. About a month after you take the test, this packet will be sent to the colleges and agencies of your choice. One copy for you and one for your counselor will be sent to your high school. The Profile contains your scores on the four academic tests and a composite score. Because ACT emphasizes that the assessment is designed to help you as well as the colleges, your report will also send you some information (in abbreviated form) regarding admissions policies, costs, special programs, etc. of the colleges of your choice. One interesting feature: it will tell you your percentile rank in relation to students who majored in education, business administration, liberal arts, and engineering, and in relation to all freshmen who took the exam in the previous three years. It will also tell you the percentage of students who attained your score who got a C or better in each of these areas—at the institution to which you've applied. Similar predictions will also be made for several specific courses.

The tests themselves are given on Saturday mornings in October, November, February, April, and June. (For those who cannot take the tests on Saturday for religious or other reasons, other special dates are available.) For a basic test fee of $7.50, you can take the four tests during a three-hour session and have the scores sent to three colleges. For $1 per report, you can specify three additional schools. ACT provides a limited number of fee waivers for economically disadvantaged students.

The tests themselves comprise four sections. The English Usage Test (40 minutes) consists of passages that may contain errors in grammar or construction; you can choose one of a number of listed alternatives or indicate NO CHANGE. The Mathematics Usage Test (50 minutes) is very similar to the math test of the SAT. The Social Studies Reading Test (35 minutes) is largely a reading-comprehension test, with the passages drawn from such social studies fields as history, political science, economics, sociology, anthropology, and psychology. The Natural Sciences Reading Test (35 minutes) is similar except that the passages are drawn from the natural sciences. What distinguishes these two reading tests from any standard reading-comprehension test is that, in addition to testing your ability to understand what you read, you may have to apply skills that you learned in these subject areas. In both the Social Studies Reading Test and the Natural Sciences Reading Test, there are *some* questions that are unrelated to the reading selections; these are similar to the traditional subject matter multiple-choice questions that appear on subject achievement tests, and you will have to draw upon your knowledge of the subjects.

The grading differs from that in the SAT in that there is no penalty for guessing—so leave as few blanks as possible. The ACTP literature points out that you shouldn't be discouraged if you don't know all the answers, because "one-half of the students tested know fewer than one-half of the answers."

Like ETS, the ACTP informs applicants that coaching or special preparation are not advised because "little specific knowledge is tested." This assertion is probably more true for the English Usage Test than for the others. For the three subject area tests (math, social studies, and natural sciences), proper review and long-term coaching *can* be a big help.

The Law School Admission Test (LSAT)

If you have any plans to apply to a law school, the chances are that you'll be required to take the LSAT some Saturday in February, April, July, October, or December. The test, produced by ETS, takes all morning (215 minutes actual testing time). A few years ago you would have had to spend all day on the LSAT and a writing ability test, which is now built into the LSAT itself.

You should be aware that the form changes from one administration of the test to the next, and that any description of the test is tentative. A few years ago, for example, the LSAT included a Figure Classification section which had a low correlation with any other part of the test and which seems to have had little to do with legal ability. A typical LSAT includes items (and sometimes a whole section) for experimental purposes—that is, such items will not be used in calculating your score, but are tryouts for future tests.

Here's how one recent LSAT shapes up.

The *logical reasoning* section deals with such skills as recognizing the point of an argument, recognizing assumptions, drawing conclusions from given evidence, inferring missing material, applying principles, identifying methods of argument, evaluating arguments, differentiating between fact and opinion, analyzing evidence, and weighing claims. The language is not overly technical, and you don't have to know formal logic.

The *practical judgment* section presents you with problem situations (usually in rather long selections, between 1,000 and 1,500 words), from which you are asked to evaluate data or apply data. In the first type of question, you have to identify major objectives, major factors, minor factors, major assumptions, and unimportant issues from a number of options dealing with the selection. The data application type asks you to use the information given to you (often in table or chart form) to answer questions and make judgments about the situation.

The *quantitative reasoning* section is designed to test your ability to deal with numbers and quantities. One recent form deals with *quantitative comparison;* you're asked to compare two given quantities in terms of relative size (or to decide if there isn't enough information to make such a judgment). The emphasis is on shortcuts in computation, since only comparative size is asked, not exact figures. Because geometric figures aren't drawn to scale, you can't guess on the basis of appearance alone. Coaching can be very useful for this section, especially if you've been away from math for a time.

The *principles and cases* section seems to be most closely correlated with legal education. It focuses on two basic skills: reading comprehension and logical reasoning. Situations are presented in which principles of law must be applied to a statement of a situation. Don't worry about the law principles; they are *given* to you (they may be real or fictitious), and you are instructed to accept them as valid and apply them logically. Don't try to substitute what you think you know about law.

The *writing ability* sections are now built into the morning test. They include a section on *error recognition* (you have to recognize and identify specific language errors: poor diction, verbosity, faulty grammar); a section on *sentence correction* (in which you substitute correct options for errors); and one on *usage* (pretty much the same thing with an extended selection). The writing ability sections don't seem to add much to the predictive validity of the test.

The LSAT differs from some of the other ETS exams in that there is no penalty for guessing.

Does the test do what it's supposed to do? The predictive validity of the LSAT is only moderate. One reviewer of an earlier LSAT form wrote in the *Mental Measurements Yearbook* that, "No attention is given to success in a law career beyond training. Considerable evidence indicates that test scores will not be related to later life success." And some of the subtests seem to have very little predictive validity for law school grades.

Reliability coefficients, too, are only moderate; for some of the subtests, they are quite low. In other words, your score depends a good deal on the particular form for which you happen to be sitting.

Your $14 fee covers one free report to a law school that you designate when you apply. But be aware that that school will also receive up to three previous scores if you took the test before. If you are worried about a possible low score, report some survivors, *don't* take advantage of the free score; you can have your score sent out later, for a small fee—after you've had a chance to see how you did (800 is top score). A number of devices have been reported for avoiding the reporting of low scores. You can cancel scores if you think you didn't do well, either at the end of the test or in writing within five days of the time you took it; if you want to cancel, do *both* to be sure. Be aware, though, that if you did indicate a school to be sent your score, that school will be notified that you asked not to have your score reported. One testwise veteran says, "Don't designate a school when you sign up; wait until you see your grade. Keep taking the test until you get a good one. But don't rush to have that one sent either; remember, the school will also get your last two scores. So sign up two more times, and either cancel or don't show. That way, only your good score will show up. Why didn't you show? You wanted to raise your score, but didn't feel well those days." Warning: a suspicious dean or admissions officer can ask ETS to check back, but most don't because of the time and effort involved.

Does coaching help? ETS says it doesn't, and for the most part they're probably right. But some coaching schools guarantee a return of fee if you don't raise your score by 70 or more points the second time around; test familiarity probably plays a role, but some test-takers report that schools have helped them to deal with LSAT definitions, which they reported weren't very clear.

The College Level Examination Program (CLEP) and the Proficiency Examination Program (PEP)

The College Level Examination Program was established by ETS in 1965 to provide a way for those outside of "the mainstream of college education" to certify their knowledge, skills, and abilities. It was designed to develop a national system of placement and credit by examination, no matter how or where an individual acquired his or her education or competencies. It is reminiscent of the "external examinations" popular in European universities during the nineteenth century, in which self-prepared candidates presented themselves for examination to get college degrees and to qualify for university (specialized or professional school) entrance.

There are two types of CLEP exams:

• A battery of five college level General Examinations in basic liberal arts areas: English composition, humanities, math, natural sciences, and social sciences/history. The lengths change from time to time; as of 1978 they are one-hour tests, except for English composition, which is 90 minutes long. Starting in June 1978, the English composition test is offered in two versions, one a combination of objective and essay tests and the other all objective. If you're pretty good at writing, choose the essay form.

• Subject examinations are available for a large number of subjects usually taught in college. In 1977–1978 there were 50 such tests offered. Each exam contains a 90-minute objective test and some are supplemented by an optional essay test. These essays are not scored by ETS, but are sent, ungraded, to the college of your choice.

Though you can take individual General Examinations (at $20 each), most candidates apply for all five, at the economy rate of $40. For the battery, expect to spend two half-day sessions, three hours in the morning and two in the afternoon. The test itself is offered the third week of each month at participating colleges and universities. Candidates who are not associated with a specific college or who don't know to which college they want to apply can take the test at any of more than 1,000 test centers. If you've been away from school for a long time and

85

are worried about how well you'll do, you can have the scores sent to you alone.

The CLEP exams have achieved a respected place in the system of higher education. Almost 2,000 colleges now accept CLEP credits as an alternative to freshman or sophomore courses in many subjects. In addition, over 750,000 individuals have taken the General Examinations through the United States Armed Forces Institute (USAFI) correspondence course program; and many students already enrolled in colleges have taken subject examinations as part of their own colleges' testing programs.

Each college makes its own decision about how it will evaluate the test scores. It may grant you general credits or specific credits (excusing you from introductory courses). It may demand certain scores in order to grant credit, and decide how many credits you will be allowed. However, ETS provides colleges with a good deal of information as a basis for evaluating the scores. For example, ETS provides norms based on the scores achieved by college students who had taken the courses on which the exams are based; it provides "scaled norms" that show the average scores earned by those who received A's and B's, and so on; there are also norms based on the number of courses taken in related fields. In addition, each General Examination is reported in subscores to show areas of strength and weakness.

Some interesting uses of the CLEP tests have been reported. For example, Florida Atlantic University started a program for admitting high school graduates directly to upper division work on the basis of good high school grades and high CLEP scores; once admitted, their upper division work was to last three years instead of the usual junior and senior years. A growing number of employers and government agencies have found CLEP tests useful in ascertaining the educational level of applicants or employees who haven't had traditional college study. And a small number of institutions have begun to grant degrees on the basis of CLEP scores alone, without any residential study. If you're interested, write to:

Board for State Academic Awards, 340 Capitol Avenue, Hartford, Connecticut 16115

Thomas A. Edison College, Forrestal Center, Forrestal Road, Princeton, New Jersey 08540

Regents External Degrees, 99 Washington Avenue, Albany, New York 12210

Some facts and figures:

• The basic standardization group on which the CLEP General Examinations were normed in 1963 consisted of a sample of 2,582 sophomores from 180 colleges, each of whom took the English composition test and one other on a systematic rotation basis. The standardized mean score was set at 500 and the standard deviation at 100. In addition, separate norms were obtained for college freshmen and seniors and for men and women in each group. (The men did better in natural sciences, math, and social sciences/history, and the women did better in English composition and humanities.)

• There is evidence of a correlation between length of schooling and scores on the CLEP; that is, the longer students have been in college, the higher their scores are likely to be. Interestingly enough, though, the test scores don't correlate nearly as well with the grades students get in their courses. One of Buros' reviewers suggests that maybe "repeated administrations of the CLEP may provide a better measure of the student's educational progress than his actual course grades."

• There is a relationship between age and test scores. The USAFI sample in 1965–1966 found that in all of the General Examinations, candidates in their early twenties did far better than those in their thirties, probably because they were closer to their years of formal education. In addition, many older test-takers hadn't had as much schooling (many had been in their teens during the Depression, and many had dropped out of school or failed to go on to college). But on all the tests except math, the scores went up sharply for those in the late thirties and older. Those over 40 scored highest of all the test-takers in social sciences/history and in humanities; apparently, knowledge in these areas keeps increasing with life experience. Knowledge of math declines from age 24 on, apparently because most adults forget what they had learned and have no reason to keep up.

• The reliability of the General Examinations is above .90, which means that whatever they measure, they're consistent in measuring it. The reliability of the subject examinations is somewhat lower, about .85.

• Benjamin Bloom, a pioneer in test reform, thinks that the tests are "praise-worthy and even exciting" in their concept. But he is less happy at finding that 60% of the CLEP questions he examined appeared to be testing for specific memorized data. "It is clear," he wrote in the *Mental Measurements Yearbook,* "that . . . these examinations lag somewhat behind modern examination practices, even if they are up-to-date with what is being taught in a random assortment of colleges and universities." The exams do fit in pretty well with what is taught in most schools, and studies show that CLEP students do as well in college as those of comparable ability who take the traditional courses.

The CLEP tests are among the few reward-oriented tests in which you have far more to gain than to lose. They're well worth trying if you think you know anything about the basic academic subjects—or even some of the specific business or technical subjects such as Business Management, Introductory Accounting, Computers and Data Processing, Human Growth and Development, Dental Materials, Oral Radiography, Microbiology, and lots more. (There's even one on Tests and Measurements.) Check with the guidance counselor at your local high school or with the admissions office at a nearby college for additional information and for a list of exams. Or write to:

College Level Examinations Program, Box 1812, Princeton, New Jersey 08540

College Level Examinations Program, Box 1903, Radio City Station, New York, New York 10019

One of the ETS regional offices (look in the telephone book if you live in one of these cities): New York City; Bethlehem, PA; Evanston, IL; Waltham, MA; Hato Rey, PR; Atlanta, GA; Austin, TX; Palo Alto, CA; or Denver, CO.

A similar program is administered by the American College Testing Program. The ACT Proficiency Examination Program (PEP), established in 1976, consists of 47 examinations designed to let students gain official recognition for learning acquired outside the classroom. Each examination is designed to measure knowledge and competencies that a person might gain through work experience in such fields as accounting, nursing, and criminal investigation, or through independent reading and study, as in educational psychology, health, or literature. ACT publishes a *PEP List of Participating Institutions,* so that you can find not only which colleges and universities will accept PEP test scores for credit, but how much credit you can expect from each. For information, write or call:

The American College Testing Program, 2201 North Dodge Street, P. O. Box 168, Iowa City, Iowa 52240, (319) 356-3711

One of the regional offices (look in the phone book under ACT Program) if you live in Portland, OR; Sacramento, CA; Broomfield, CO; Austin, TX; Manhattan, KA; Springfield, MO; Hinsdale, IL; Wheeling, IL; Bowling Green, OH; Tallahassee, FL; Atlanta, GA; or King of Prussia, PA.

7.
The Verbal
Aptitude Tests

The standardized scholastic aptitude tests have mushroomed on the educational landscape since World War II. A series of events account for the rapid development of such tests: the postwar baby boom; young Americans' increasing demands for higher education so that they, too, could get a share of the pie; government support for college education for veterans and minorities; and industry's need for trained personnel. Faced with increasing pressure for a limited number of spaces, colleges and universities expanded; but many of the private colleges, especially, have looked for ways of limiting access to those they consider the most "promising" candidates. In the process, many capable and competent students may be screened out, often because they haven't learned the skill of taking tests.

This chapter is *not* a review or practice chapter. You can get old tests and practice tests from a number of sources. You can also use the familiarization materials that are sent out by the test publishers, or you can buy books of practice problems and questions.

The purpose of this chapter is *not* to drill you on vocabulary or grammar or rules of writing. Again, if you need this kind of review, there are companies that specialize in publishing review books.

This chapter is designed to help you develop test-taking strategies in general. It will explore general approaches to the basic types of questions that you may find on verbal sections of many scholastic aptitude tests.

KEEPING YOUR ANSWERS STRAIGHT

You probably wouldn't believe the number of people who *know* the correct answer on a standardized test—and *mark* the wrong one. This happens for two basic reasons: *thinking* error and *marking* error.

Thinking error comes in three basic shapes.

• *You confused the directions.* For example, you might have been told to identify an *error* and instead you chose the answer you thought was *true*. If you don't remember that *true* and *correct* are not synonyms, review the section on test instructions in Chapter 3.

• *You mixed answers and symbols.* For example: you worked out a math problem and know the correct answer is 3. But when you look over the options— (1) 3 (2) 7 (3) 21 (4) 32—you chose (3) instead of (1). Or you know that the answer to a question is *Albany,* so you chose (A) for Albany, even though option (A) was Kalamazoo.

• *You inverted letters or digits.* After struggling through a problem, you calculated an answer of 247 that checks out. But you marked the option for 274.

Marking error has to do with the mechanics of marking your answer on the answer sheet. You've probably taken a lot of electronically graded tests before. So have most of those other folks to whom a funny thing happened on their way to the wrong end of a normal curve. They forgot that machines don't make the fine distinctions that human readers can make: between stray marks and wrong answers, or between tentative answers and considered choices, or between an *almost* erased first impression and a final choice.

There are several forms in which these answer sheets are presented. In all of them, you fill in the space for the correct answer in the row corresponding with the same number question.

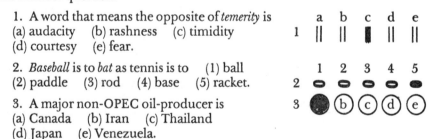

1. A word that means the opposite of *temerity* is (a) audacity (b) rashness (c) timidity (d) courtesy (e) fear.

2. *Baseball* is to *bat* as tennis is to (1) ball (2) paddle (3) rod (4) base (5) racket.

3. A major non-OPEC oil-producer is (a) Canada (b) Iran (c) Thailand (d) Japan (e) Venezuela.

The basic rules on the mechanics:

• Use *only* the special pencil provided; this pencil makes marks that create the necessary electrical contact.

• Make your marks *heavy* and *black,* and be sure they are within the lines or ovals provided.

- If you change your mind, erase your previous answer *completely*. Leave no electrical contact marks behind.
- Mark only *one* space for an answer. In most tests, marking more than one will leave you with *no* credit.
- Avoid stray marks on the paper. Don't tap, mark a space .o come back to, or do any calculation on the answer sheet. The machine can't distinguish between such marks and actual answers.
- Keep your answer sheet close to the question booklet, so that you don't have to shift papers for each answer.
- Make sure that the answer you fill in is for the same number as that for the question on which you've been working.

WORD MEANINGS

The vocabulary section of a verbal test is based on the assumption that you can't do scholastic work very well without a grasp of the major tools of the trade: words. In fact, because any mass test depends on words, vocabulary is the best single indicator on group tests of what is called "intelligence" or "ability" or "aptitude."

Vocabulary tests can run the gamut. Straight definitions can be presented in the form: "Which choice most nearly means. . . ?" or the instructions can call for antonyms. Or you may be given a sentence and asked to choose words to insert in numbered blanks. Or you can be asked to find appropriate analogies from among groups of words—the most sophisticated type of vocabulary question. In fact, it is usually used as a test of *reasoning* ability rather than a test of word knowledge. For that reason, we'll deal with verbal analogies in a separate section.

Synonyms and antonyms are usually asked as straightforward denotative (dictionary definition) questions. For example:

> **Directions:** Each question below consists of a word in capital letters followed by five lettered words or phrases. Choose the lettered word or phrase that is most nearly *the same* in meaning as the word in capital letters.

REDRESS: (a) correct   (b) repeat   (c) change   (d) duplicate   (e) redoubt

FORSWEAR: (a) offend   (b) persuade   (c) oppose   (d) perjure   (e) affirm

PRODIGIOUS: (a) childlike   (b) extraordinary   (c) heroic   (d) clever   (e) wasteful

QUERULOUS: (a) talkative   (b) inquisitive   (c) complaining   (d) searching   (e) illegal

Antonyms, of course, would involve choosing the word or phrase that is most nearly *opposite* in meaning as the word in capital letters. Synonym and antonym questions may appear in a variety of forms. For example:

When one is *prodigal,* he or she is: (a) wayward (b) lost (c) niggardly
(d) redeemed (e) extravagant.
or:
Select the pair of words that are *opposite* in meaning.
(a) uncouth: vicious
(b) credulous: skeptical
(c) partisan: supporter
(d) obdurate: stubborn
(e) susceptible: exposed

Generally, of course, the larger your working vocabulary, the more likely
you are to do well in this kind of test. But even if you know and use a large number
of words, you can fall into some traps—mainly those of carelessness or confusion.
And even if you don't recognize a word immediately, don't give up: many words
can be thought through by using elements that you know or can figure out. Don't
fall into the low scorer trap of assuming you don't know something just because
you don't recognize it immediately. True, in professionally made standardized
tests you're not likely to find all those clues and giveaways you can count on in
classroom tests; so you'll have to stretch your reasoning ability. Here are some
strategies and suggestions.

Be familiar with prefix and suffix forms. More than half the words in English
are combinations of common terms in Latin or Greek, and many more come from
German. As the language grew, many old words were combined to form new ones.
If you know the common prefixes and suffixes, you will be able to figure out the
meaning of many unfamiliar words. For example, the word *hyperopia* may be new
to you. But if you know that *hyper-* is a common prefix that means *over,* or *beyond* the
ordinary (think of *hyperactive*), you should be able to limit your choices. An option
that relates to sight should ring a bell (*myopia* means *nearsightedness*), and you should
figure out that *hyperopia* probably means *farsightedness.* At the end of this chapter is a
list of some of the major prefixes and suffixes. It pays to learn them, because each
one may open up the meanings of scores of words you don't recognize. (Don't
waste your time trying to memorize vocabulary lists; you can't make up in a short
time what you missed all those years.)

Think of other words having similar prefixes or suffixes. What if you *didn't* know
the meaning of *hyper-?* Don't panic. What words begin with *hyper-?* (Don't confuse
it with *hypo-,* which means precisely the opposite.) There's *hypertension,* for example,
and *hypercritical,* and *hyperactive* and *hyperkinetic.* What meaning do they suggest?
Let's try another example:

Micrology means: (a) an instrument for measuring light (b) the study
of microbes (c) attention to small details (d) small living organisms

Even if you don't know what *micro-* means, you should recognize it as the
beginning of *microscope*—an instrument for viewing things (as in *telescope* and
periscope); so *micro-* must refer to the *kinds* of things one sees with a microscope—
small things. Therefore, option (a) is eliminated immediately. Option (b) sounds

too much like the stem word (see the hint below on similar-sounding options). This leaves (c) and (d).

Here, you apply the same process to the suffixes. The suffix *-ology* is a familiar one in school; it means the study of or attention to (as in *biology, geology,* and *psychology*); it isn't likely that it would be used to describe organisms. So by reasoning alone, you should be able to choose (c) as the correct option.

Be alert to definitions of similar-sounding words. A common trap is an option with the definition of a word that sounds very much like the stem word. In an earlier example, you may have noticed that one of the choices for *querulous* was *talkative. Querulous* means *complaining,* but *talkative* would be the synonym for *garrulous.* If you read the item quickly and carelessly, you might have confused the two.

Here's another example:

Prodigy means the same as   (a) marvel   (b) hopeful   (c) wayward
(d) spendthrift   (e) returned

As you look over the definitions, you could easily be confused by a synonym for *prodigal,* which means *spendthrift.* But a second kind of error can occur if you read the word carelessly, and if you're not really sure of the meaning of prodigal. If you have a dim recollection of the story of the Prodigal Son, and you use a hazy kind of association, you might also pick *wayward*—or even *returned.* The point is that both kinds of errors in this case would flow out of your confusion of the two words. Actually, a *prodigy* is a wonder or a marvel.

If the definition fits a word that is similar in sound to the stem word, reject it. Examples of some similar-sounding words with quite different meanings: anteprohibition/anti-prohibition; faction/fraction; imprecate/implicate; explicate/extricate.

Be wary of options that sound very much like the stem word. Synonyms and antonyms rarely sound very much like the stem word—and if they did, the test-maker would not be likely to use them. For example:

Faction means most nearly the same as   (a) clique   (b) fiction   (c) part
(d) element   (e) function

This item was deliberately loaded with common traps (by the way, professional test-makers don't use traps—they use "attractive distractors"). Option (b) is included because it sounds like the stem word; only the most naive test-taker would choose it. Option (c) is a trap because it defines a word (fraction) that is very similar in sound to the stem word. So does option (d) (factor). And option (e) sounds like the stem word. *Faction* is a synonym for *clique.*

Try alternative meanings and uses. You may find yourself frustrated because you know the meaning of the word but can't find the option that should fit. Remember that many English words have several meanings. For example:

The observer stood on the crest of a hill *overlooking* the valley, but *overlooked* the rock in front of him.

If the meaning that you anticipated doesn't appear, try using the stem word in another sense. The common word *call,* for example, could mean to summon; to invite; to read over a list; to announce with authority (as to call a halt); to bid, to invoke; to rouse from sleep; to attract animals by using imitations; to communicate by telephone; to convoke, as with a meeting; to demand payment; to summon to duty; to give a name to; to describe (as in "it's called a good restaurant"); to shout; to muster; to collect; to decide or referee (as in "call the shot"). And we haven't even touched the meanings of the word in noun form! So if you don't see your first choice, don't panic. Go over the possibilities systematically and see if there are other choices that fit.

Sentence completion is another common word-meaning exercise. This type of verbal ability item calls on you not only to know the denotative (or dictionary) meaning of the words involved, but to grasp the meaning of the whole sentence and to be familiar with the *usage* of the words. Because there are more elements involved, it may be more difficult than the word-matching types. But you also have one tremendous advantage: you can use contextual clues. Therefore a sentence completion comes closer to what you actually do when you come across an unfamiliar word in real life.

The form of the sentence-completion items may vary from one standardized test to another, but here is the way they often appear:

> Directions: Each sentence below has one or two blanks, each blank indicating that something has been omitted. Beneath the sentence are five lettered words or sets of words. Choose the word or set of words that *best* fits the meaning of the sentence as a whole.
>
> 1. From a morose and cynical rebel, he was _____ into a stalwart _____ of religion and a roaring reactionary in politics.
> (a) transformed, critic   (b) converted, defender   (c) demoted, bulwark
> (d) elevated, opponent

In dealing with sentence-completion types, all of the hints listed earlier are useful. In addition, you have contextual clues. But such clues are not accidental; they are *deliberately* inserted in the passage to point to *only* one set of words as the appropriate one. Usually, each word will make sense in a *section* of the sentence, but the point is to have the entire sentence make sense when seen as a whole.

In selection 1 you were told that an individual was changed in some way; the wording suggests a *reversal* of role. Neither *demoted* nor *elevated* carries through this connotation, so you can eliminate options (c) and (d). But if he changed from being a rebel, it isn't likely that he would be a *critic* of religion—certainly not if the change made him a political reactionary. So choice (b) would be the logical one after the systematic elimination of the others.

Let's try another:

2. E. L. Kelley's finding in 1964 that grades on a state board exam to license physicians _____ less than .20 with a national board exam in the same subject, or with the grades earned in that subject the previous year, must _____ that the state board was a bad measuring instrument.
(a) correlate, suggest   (b) conflict, demonstrate   (c) match, conclude
(d) reflect, advise

Often your choice reflects your recollection that some combinations of words go together. In reading this book, you have seen the word *correlate* used frequently in connection with a percentage figure. If nothing else, choice (a) sounds best, although some of the others might make sense. One of the purposes of this kind of exercise is to find if you're sensitive to combinations that fit *better* than others.

READING COMPREHENSION

Reading-comprehension exercises have become a standard feature of most scholastic aptitude tests, from early elementary placement tests to graduate school admissions exams. (For example, half the time on the GRE verbal test is devoted to reading comprehension; the bulk of the LSAT is reading comprehension; and three of the four sections of the ACT exam deal in whole or in part with reading comprehension.) They are based on the finding that success in school is closely tied with the ability to understand what you read.

There are several types of reading-comprehension questions, all handled differently, so it's important to know the kind (or kinds) that you're facing. For this reason, on many tests you should disregard the usual instruction to read the passage carefully before answering any of the questions. *Read the questions first!* Don't get involved in the complexities of the passage before you know what is being asked of you. If you're taking one of the better-prepared standardized tests, like the SAT or the GRE or the ACT, skimming won't be enough. But it may be for the bulk of the aptitude tests on the market. The decision will depend on which of the types of questions you'll have to answer. These basic types appear on all reading-comprehension exercises, although the level of sophistication and the "mix" will vary.

Recognition types are the easiest to handle. By and large, they measure skim-and-match skills rather than real understanding. There are two basic types of recognition questions, also known as *explicit* questions.

The "main-idea question" often asks you to identify what a passage is "about." Main-idea questions may appear in the following forms:

A title that best expresses the idea of this passage is:
The writer's basic theme is:
This anecdote may best be described as:
• The selection illustrates:

The author's purpose is to:
The main idea of the selection is:

In many junior high and senior high school achievement tests, main-idea questions may be surprisingly obvious. Here's a sample from one standardized test of "reading and literature." Following a passage, the test-taker is asked:

This passage is about   (a) baseball   (b) football   (c) stamina
(d) courage.

Another question on the same test asks the test-taker to identify a selection as a poem, short story, play, novel, or jingle!

For a straight main-idea question, skimming is all that is really necessary. (That's why main-idea types are preferred to show how rapidly you can read after having taken a speed reading course.) The point is to identify the central theme and separate it from illustrative or supporting material. This central theme may be summarized in a topic sentence, but unlike the "topic sentence" style you may have been taught in English class, this summary sentence may appear anywhere in the passage.

You should be aware that some of the more sophisticated tests like the SAT, the GRE, or the ACT often use questions that *look* like main-idea questions but are actually *inferential* questions. (We'll deal with them shortly.) However, even on such exams, you may find main-idea questions. For example, one of the four questions illustrating SAT reading-comprehension items in recent familiarization materials begins, "The passage deals mainly with the. . . ," followed by five choices. But because such questions will be mixed in with other types, skimming won't be enough.

The detail question, the other basic form of recognition question, focuses on a specific name or fact. One of the reviews in the *Mental Measurements Yearbook* deals with a junior high school test in which students are presented with a passage from Mark Twain's story of the cat and the pain-killer in *The Adventures of Tom Sawyer.* Writes the reviewer, "One would expect an item on what was the point of the episode, or what Aunt Polly learned from it. Not so; the question asks for the name of the cat." In apparent disgust, the reviewer concludes, "Once you know what, in general, a selection is about, who wrote it, the names of the principal characters, and whether it is a short story, poem, play, etc., you are likely to get a high score."

For the lower grades, the appropriate detail will be obvious—often taken verbatim from the selection. On the college or graduate school admission tests, the detail question, like the main-idea question, will be on a more sophisticated level. And it will usually involve more than mere recognition. In the more advanced tests, some translation will be involved; there will be some shifting around of materials, or the use of synonyms, approximations, or equivalents. For example, in one college-entrance standardized test, in the body of a reading exercise appears the statement that "Warm-blooded animals, of necessity, have a higher metabolism rate than do cold-blooded animals because of the need to maintain body temperatures and because chemical reactions occur more rapidly at higher temperatures." One question asks:

> In contrast with cold-blooded animals, warm-blooded animals
> (a) are of a higher order
> (b) need oxygen for survival
> (c) are more adaptable
> (d) have higher energy requirements
> (e) are likely to be carnivorous

But it's still a detail question. And by skim-and-match you can locate the sentence in which the answer appears, just as with the junior high school question about the name of the cat.

Finding implications and drawing inferences are two sides of the same process. A reader *infers* from a passage what the writer *implies* or suggests without actually saying it. Sometimes the inferential question is straightforward: "We can infer from the passage that. . . ." More often, it is suggested by such words as *probably, apparently, might, most likely, indicates,* and *suggests.* And sometimes an inferential question reads like a straight detail question: "The lawyer nodded his head because. . . ."

The difference between this and a detail question is that the reason the lawyer nodded is *not* written out in a specific phrase or sentence; you have to infer it from the rest of the passage. Because there are different ways of dealing with the detail question (skim-and-match) and the inferential question (analytical reading), you should be able to identify each type quickly. If the test is loaded with inferential questions (as in the Law School Admission Test, for example), it would certainly be safe to assume that many items that look like detail questions are likely to be inferential questions.

Inferential questions can deal with a wide variety of materials and specifics. You may be asked to read a passage and infer the definition of a word with which you are unfamiliar ("A *hoatzin* is probably a   (a) snake   (b) bird   (c) fish   (d) machine   (e) person"). You may be asked to interpolate (figure out a missing part) or extrapolate (project or predict). For example, "Assuming that the situation does not change during the next decade, which of the following actions is Congress likely to take?" A common type asks you to draw conclusions from the information given you. A sample ACT item* presents summaries of four experiments conducted with bats, and the findings in each case. A typical question is:

> Which conclusion, if any, can be drawn from Experiment 4?
> (A) Bats evidently use some sort of radar to guide themselves.
> (B) The presence of radar waves has no apparent effect on the bats.
> (C) The presence of radar waves confuses the bats by obstructing their natural means of locating obstacles.
> (D) None of the above.

---

*Copyright 1978 by the American College Testing Program. Reproduced by permission.

Inferential questions may ask you to identify a principle or rule that underlies a passage, or to identify a connection with a principle or rule not stated in the passage. For example, one sample GRE question based on a reading selection asks, "With which of the following aphorisms would the exploiters of the 1870's probably have been in strongest agreement?" Such inferential questions are as much tests of *reasoning* ability as of reading ability.

Questions to identify mood and purpose are inferential types you're likely to find on many general reading-comprehension tests. They focus on the writer's *mood, attitude,* or *style.* You may be asked if the writer is flippant or serious, confident or uncertain, optimistic or pessimistic. Such questions may ask about the writer's *purpose*: was the passage descriptive or sarcastic, literal or allegorical? If you understand what you read, there should usually be enough clues to provide you with the answer. Below are some of the types of questions you're likely to find in this category.

The tone of the writer is: (a) humorous   (b) solemn   (c) emotional (d) cynical   (e) matter-of-fact

The writer's attitude toward Mrs. Jessup appears to be one mainly of (a) affection   (b) pity   (c) indifference   (d) respect   (e) dislike

The writer apparently wishes to convey the impression that he (a) exercises as often as possible   (b) is a good tennis player   (c) avoids physical exertion whenever possible   (d) engages in sports to be sociable

This passage is probably taken from   (a) an encyclopedia   (b) an owner's manual   (c) a newspaper advertisement   (d) a technical report   (e) a description of one purchaser's experience

STRATEGIES FOR HANDLING READING-COMPREHENSION QUESTIONS

Again, most main-idea and detail questions are based on recognition, involve skim-and-match skills, and don't really require careful reading of the passage. But inferential questions do. The explicit recognition is more common in the tests given in the elementary grades and in junior high school than it is in those given older students. Increasingly, reading-comprehension tests given in high school and college (and for college and graduate school admissions) contain a large number of inferential questions. The reason for the difference is fairly obvious: younger children are still struggling with basic *decoding* and *translation* skills (the ability to transform the symbols into sounds, and the ability to translate from one combination of words into another); older students are expected to understand the content of a passage in a more comprehensive way. High school and college students are expected to *interpret* (find relationships between ideas), to *analyze* (break the passage down into its component parts), to *draw inferences* (use clues to reconstruct information that hasn't been given), and to *draw conclusions.* So the word *comprehension* means different things at different levels of achievement.

In general, the following suggestions should help you to cope with the various types.

- *Skim the passage first,* to get a general sense of its message. See it as a whole and focus on the main idea, even if you're not asked a specific question about it.

- *Skim the questions* to get a sense of the type of thinking you're asked to do. If even *some* of the questions are inferential, you'll have to read the passage more carefully.

- *Focus on the demands of the questions.* Even if the items are inferential, you may need to focus on only one section of the passage for each. If the question relates to the whole selection (as do mood or purpose or style questions), your decision on how carefully to read the passage will depend on how obvious the answers are.

- *Eliminate options if*:
  (1) they don't relate to the theme of the passage;
  (2) they are obvious misstatements or misinterpretations of sections of the passage;
  (3) they contradict the sense of the passage, even if *you* think they are true.

- *Go back to the reading selection as often as necessary.* Usually it shouldn't be necessary to reread the whole selection. Refer back to the portion of the selection indicated in the specific question.

- *Be alert to specific determiners* that may invalidate an otherwise true statement. Such determiners are words like *always, never, absolutely,* and *positively.* But be careful! Professionals are more likely than teachers or professors to use such words deliberately and with forethought. In such tests, specific determiners are as likely to be found in correct options as in incorrect ones.

- *Look for overspecific distractors* (options) in inferential questions. Most inferential questions are more general than similar detail questions. Many distractors deal with only *part* of the indicated response. By and large, the *more general* response is likely to be the correct answer.

VERBAL ANALOGIES

While verbal analogies are often considered tests of vocabulary, they're actually far more (although, of course, you must understand the meaning of the words involved). All analogies, verbal and math, are tests of your ability to perceive relationships and therefore are frequently used as tests of general reasoning ability. Some major tests of scholastic aptitude like the Miller Analogies Test (MAT), used to screen applicants to graduate programs, consist of nothing but analogies.

Because the relationships are often subtle, the unsophisticated test-taker usually has a good deal of trouble with analogies. Dealing with analogy problems is a skill that can be learned, but as with other complex skills, suggestions and hints alone aren't enough. Of all verbal areas, this one probably requires the greatest amount of practice. If you persist, using the suggestions listed here and in Chapter 2, you should get the hang of it. Remember the *basic* suggestion for working on test-taking skills: try to practice by thinking aloud while someone monitors you.

Verbal analogies ask you to infer the relationship between one set of words, and then to find the same relationship between words in another set. For example:

> COLLIE is to DOG as ROSE is to _____ (a) thorn   (b) geranium
> (c) plant   (d) seed   (e) petal

In this rather simple example, a *collie* is a kind of *dog*. Therefore a *rose* has to be some kind of—something. A rose *could* be a kind of flower, but *flower* is not one of the options, nor is any other word that could mean flower. *Thorn, seed,* and *petal* are all *parts* of a rose plant, but we're looking for something of which *rose* is a part or a kind. *Plant* is the obvious choice.

The form in which the analogy is presented may vary from one kind of test to another. Here is a common analogy form:

> LATENT: MANIFEST:: APTITUDE: (a) strength   (b) understanding
> (c) skill   (d) knowledge   (e) ability

If you intend to take the SAT, you'll find the following form:

> YEAST: DOUGH::   (A) smile: flirtation   (B) flirtation: friendship
> (C) flattery: conceit   (D) trust: handshake   (E) frown: smile

Here are some suggestions for dealing with analogies in general, and verbal analogies in particular.

• *Establish the relationship between the items in the first pair.* Then find the same relationship in a paired option. In the example above, yeast makes dough rise; it puffs it up. The only pair in which the same relationship holds (puffing up) is (C). But finding the relationship alone may not be enough. For example, suppose (E) were *balloon: breath.* Option (C) would still be the correct answer, because the relationship is presented *in the same order* as the model pair.

• *If more than one option contains the same relationship, you may have to refine the relationship or find another.* For example:

> LOG: BOARD::   (a) pie: cake   (b) spoon: fork   (C) iron: steel
> (d) wire: bar   (e) water: steam

A log and a board are both made of the same material: wood. But *this* relationship won't help you much, because *each* option contains items of the same material. So you have to go back to find another relationship. In this case, you might notice that a board is *made from* a log—and is a more refined form of that material. Pie and cake are independent forms in the same general category, as are spoon and fork, and wire and bar. Water and steam are reversible forms of the same material. But iron is made *into* steel, and so (c) seems to have the same relationship as the model pair.

100

Here are some of the relationships that often appear on verbal analogies.

	as in
word: synonym	commerce: trade / conflict: strife
word: antonym	accept: reject / raise: lower
whole: part	circle: arc / syllogism: premise
part: part	thumb: forefinger / bass: treble
cause: effect	bite: swelling / burn: blister
object: purpose	knife: cut / pen: write
object: user	auto: driver / lancet: surgeon
raw material: product	wool: sweater / wood: paper
less: more (degree)	slim: skinny / assertive: aggressive
less: more (size)	stream: river / brad: nail
concept: measurement	time: hour / volume: liter
genus or class: member	dog: collie / primate: chimpanzee
individual: group	sheep: flock / goose: gaggle
early stage: developed	caterpillar: butterfly / larva: chrysalis
object / subject: action	grasshopper: jump / cod: swim

grammatical relationships:

noun: adjective	cow: bovine / wolf: vulpine
singular: plural	alumnus: alumni / curriculum: curricula
male: female	bull: cow / drake: duck

• *Check the relationship between the first word of EACH pair.* Sometimes the connection between the words in the model pair is not clear. You might find a more clear-cut relationship between the *first word of each pair.* For example:

IGNORANCE: POVERTY / KNOWLEDGE::   (a) sustenance
(b) happiness   (c) entertainment   (d) wisdom   (e) schools

The relationship between ignorance and poverty may not appear clear standing alone. More likely, the relationship may not seem to be one that you can find in any of the options. So you might ask about the relationship between *ignorance* and *knowledge.* This *could* be opposites—in which case you should probably find *wealth* among the options. But it isn't. Another relationship is that ignorance is the *absence* or *lack* of knowledge. Then it becomes clear that, if the relationship is one of *deprivation,* option (a) could fit (ignorance is the *absence* of knowledge, while poverty is the *absence* of sustenance).

• *Use grammatical clues as well as logical ones.* You'll find that the correct pair has the same *grammatical* relationship as the model pair.

noun: noun / noun: _____ the correct answer must be a noun
noun: adjective / noun: _____ look for an adjective
noun: noun / adjective: _____ look for an adjective
noun: verb / noun: _____ has to be a verb

This hint may not help you much on the better professionally designed tests, in which *every* option would normally be gramatically consistent with the model. But on the poorer tests (and on some items even on the better tests) you may find that you can eliminate one or two options. In this case, as you may remember from Chapter 4, the odds favor a guess.

Many psychometricians think analogy tests are the best single indicator of general reasoning ability, but quite a few individuals in and out of the field are not so sure. In this kind of test, as in so many others, an imaginative and knowledgeable test-taker can run into trouble by perceiving an analogy that the test-*makers* did not see. This point emerges clearly in an article that appeared in the spring of 1976 in *The Chronicle of Higher Education*. Entitled "Dear Educational Testing Service," the article consisted wholly of letters from a mother to the ETS and responses from an associate examiner. The mother questioned a sample item in the SAT explanatory booklet:

> Select the lettered pair that *best* expresses a relationship similar to that expressed in the original pair.
> WANDER: TRESPASS::   (a) eat: gorge   (b) recline: sprawl
> (c) mar: destroy   (d) narrate: perjure   (e) glance: examine

The indicated answer was (d). But the mother made a case for (a) on the ground that *trespass* and *gorge* both convey the idea of sin; and that (d) *perjury* connotes a deliberate intent and an intellectual quality not present in *trespass* (or *gorge*). "My problem," the mother concluded, "seems to be how to select which answer *best* expresses the appropriate relationship. Could you please explain this?"

The exchange was revealing. The examiner began by "explaining" why the mother was mistaken, mentioned that several staff members agreed that the question was valid, and pointed out that an analysis of response patterns of test-takers showed that the higher-scoring students had answered it "correctly" (that is, as ETS wanted). "If you find that you still have problems with the question," the examiner concluded, "please do not hesitate to write to me."

The mother persisted. She cited dictionary definitions to support her argument that *trespass* and *gorge* both connote excessiveness, just as *trespass* and *perjure* both connote illegality. "You indicate that this question is one of the more difficult ones," she wrote. "I would say that it is difficult not because of its substance, but because it is tricky." In a P.S., she added:

> Perhaps I should explain that my hang-up on word tests may stem from a traumatic experience in first grade. As a pre-reading exercise the class was asked to draw words read aloud by the teacher. The word I remember was flau(-a)r. Every student other than myself drew something akin to a daisy and I drew a sack with x's. It was marked wrong.

At the conclusion, the examiner conceded that the mother had a point, admitted that the question "may well appear ambiguous to some," and promised that "we shall delete it from our [sample] materials."

The exchange produced a number of letters from readers. "The major concern of people reading the ETS letters," wrote one reader, "is probably not so much one of content as it is one of *attitude*. . . . How much trust can one maintain in an institution which responds defensively to clearly valid criticism, whose attitude is 'Here's why we are right,' rather than, 'How did we manage to miss this point?' " The writer went on to note that the question "was grudgingly removed from the sample booklet." But, he asked, "what of the hundreds of questions on the *actual* tests. . . ? The iceberg has been manicured so that its tip is no longer visible and we are asked to believe that . . . it is no longer dangerous."

A professor at the University of Iowa wrote: "It is almost amusing to see the E.T.S. plunging so blithely into the troubled waters of analogy, which have given philosophers the shivers for years. . . . The real tragedy, of course, is with those people who are creative enough to take unusual perspectives on the world. For they often find E.T.S.-type tests impossible to master."

But a research associate at the University of Kentucky thought that the mother had missed the issue on *how* one takes such a test. "The critical point," he wrote, "is to ignore completely the question of locating the correct answer, and instead to give the answer that the composer of the test thinks is correct," presumably by using test-taking strategies instead of applying knowledge of a subject. "I have done very well on many standardized tests," he concluded, "but I have given the answer *I* thought to be correct only when all other methods of analysis have failed."

PREFIXES YOU SHOULD KNOW

The following list contains common prefixes that occur in many English words. If you know the meanings of each of the prefixes listed here, you should be able to figure out the meanings of hundreds of words you don't recognize. Try to figure out the meaning of each of the sample words, and then use your dictionary to check your answer (and to find additional examples).

	Meaning	*Examples*
a-	not, without	atypical, amoral, atonal
ab-	away from	abnormal, abduct, abjure
ad-	to, toward	admit, adhere, admixture
ambi-	both	ambidextrous, ambivalent, ambiguous
amphi-	around	amphitheatre, amphigean
an-	not, without	anarchy, anemia, anesthesia
ante-	before	antebellum, antedate, antediluvian, antemeridian
anti-	against, opposite	antibody, anticathode, antiaircraft, anticlimax
aqua-	water	aquaduct, aquatic, aquaplane
arch-	first, chief	archetype, archbishop, archeology

auto-	self	autobiography, automobile, autocracy, autogenesis
ben- bene-	good, well	benefactor, beneficial, benevolent
bi-	two	bicameral, biped, bicycle
bio-	life	biology, biography, biopsy, biogenesis
com- con-	together with	confide, commune, combine, compose, concur, condescend
contra-	against	contradict, contrary, contraindication
de-	away from, down from	deduct, debase, descent, decant, decadence
dia-	across, through	diameter, diagonal, diagram
dis-	apart, not	disparate, disillusion, disclaim, disavow, disenchant, disapprove
dys-	hard, ill, bad	dyscrasia, dyspepsia, dystrophy
ec- ect- ecto-	out of, from	eccentric, eclectic, ectype, ectoplasm, ectoparasite
endo-	within	endocardiac, endoskeleton, endoscope
epi-	over	epidermis, epicenter, epidemic
eu-	good, well, agreeable	euphemism, eulogy, eugenic, eupeptic
ex-	out of, beyond	expel, external, exterior, extirpate
extra-	beyond, besides, outside of	extraordinary, extrahazardous, extraterritorial
hyper-	over, beyond	hypertension, hypercritical, hyperkinetic
hypo-	less, under	hypodermic, hypogenous
in-	in, into	incorporate, incarnate, incase
in-	not	insensitive, inadequate, inept, inarticulate, ineffective
inter-	between, among	intercontinental, intermontane, interregnum, intersect
mis-	less, not, wrong	misadventure, misconstrue, misbehave, misbegotten, miscarry
mon- mono-	one, single, alone	monopoly, monarchy, monograph, monolith, monogamy
non-	not	noninterference, nonattendance, nonresistance
omni-	all	omnivorous, omnipotent, omniscient
per-	through	perceive, perennial, permeate

poly-	many, much	polygamy, polyglot, polygon, polyphonic, polygenesis
pre-	before	predict, predate, prejudice, predispose
pro-	forward, toward	project, probiscus, proceed
re-	again, back	recede, regress, relapse, rebut, recant, recall
retro-	backward	retrogress, retrospect, retroactive
semi-	half	semicircle, semiannual, semidiurnal, semi-opaque
sub-	under	sublet, substation, submarine, subterranean, subservient, subordinate
super-	above, over, beyond	superfluous, superannuate, supernatural, superintend
syn-	with	synchronous, syndicate, synthesis
tele-	far	telescope, television, telephone
trans-	across	transcontinental, transoceanic, transport, transcribe, transfer
tri-	three	triad, tricycle, tripartite
ultra-	beyond	ultraviolet, ultramarine
un-	not	unsettle, unruly, unproductive

...AND SUFFIXES YOU SHOULD KNOW

-able -ible	capable of	portable, legible, credible
-ac -ic	pertaining to	cardiac, dramatic, poetic
-cle -cul -cule	small	molecule, follicle, miniscule, corpuscle
-cy	condition, state of	obstinacy, captaincy, aristocracy
-ic	making, made	soporific, frantic, manic
-il -ile	capable of, condition	docile, mobile, ductile, nubile
-ise -ize	to make	mineralize, baptize, chastise
-logy	science of, study of, attention to	philology, biology, geology
-spect	look	inspect, circumspect

...AND SOME ROOT WORDS THAT CAN GO ANYWHERE

anim	mind, soul, breath	animal, animate, unanimous
ann enn	year	annual, biennial, semi-annual, perennial
anthrop	man	anthropology, misanthrope, philanthropy, anthropomorphic
arch	first, rule, government	monarch, anarchy, oligarchy
aud(i) audit	hear	audible, audition, audience
bell(i)	war	belligerent, bellicose, rebellious, antebellum
biblio	book	bibliography, bibliophile, Bible
breve	short	abbreviate, brevity
cap	take	capacious, capture, capable
cent	one hundred	century, centennial, centigrade
chron(os)	time	chronology, synchrony, chronicle, anachronism
corpus	body	corpse, corporeal, incorporate
cred	believe	credibility, credulity, credence, incredible
demo(s)	people	democracy, demagogue, epidemic
derm	skin	epiderm(is), hypodermic, dermatology
di diur	day	diary, diurnal, journey
dict	say	diction, dictionary, predict, dictate, dictum, verdict
duc(t)	to lead	duct, viaduct, aqueduct, induct, educate, induce
dynam	power	dynamo, dynamite, dynamic
fac(t)	to make, to do	manufacture, factory, facile
gen(er)	class, group, race	generic, genus, gender
gram graph	write, writing	telegram, Gramophone, grammar, telegraph, graphic, graphology, monograph
helio	sun	heliotrope, helium, heliotype
heter(o)	other, different	heterodox, heterogeneous, heteromorphic
homo-	same (from Greek)	homogeneous, homonym, homophone, homosexual

homo-	man (from Latin)	homocide, hominal
jur jus	law, swear	juridical, jurisprudence, abjure, jury, perjure, justice
labor	work	laboratory, collaborate, belabor, laborious
leg	law	legislate, legal, legitimate
liber	book	library, libretto, libel
lite lith	stone	monolith, lithograph, lithography; -ite is used in mineral names.
luc	light	translucent, lucid, elucidate
mal	bad, wrong	malevolent, malefactor, malady, malediction, malnutrition
man(u)	hand	manual, manufacture, manuscript, manumit
mar	sea	maritime, marine, mariner, submarine
mis mit	send	transmit, missile, admit, dismiss, manumit
mori mort	die, death	mortal, immortal, mortuary, moribund, mortify, mortgage
omni	all	omniscient, omnipotent, omnibus, omnivorous, omnipresent
orth(o)	straight, right	orthodox, orthodontist, orthopedist
pan	all	panHellenic, panAmerican, panSlavic
ped(o) pod	foot	pedestrian, podiatrist, impede, pedometer, podium
phil(e) phil(ous)	love of	bibliophile, philanthropy, Anglophile, Philadelphia, philology, philosophy
port	carry	portable, transport, portage, porter, export, import
psych	soul, mind	psychology, psychiatry, psychopath, psychoanalysis, psychometrics, psychosomatic
sci	know	science, omniscient, conscious, prescient
scrib script	write	describe, inscribe, scripture, scribe, manuscript, transcribe
secut sequi	follow	consecutive, consequence, sequence, sequel
sen(s) sent	feel	sensitive, sensibility, sentient, consensus
soma(to)	body	somatic, psychosomatic, somatogenesis, somatology

spec	look, see	spectacle, spectator, inspect, specter, spectrum
urb	city	urban, urbane, suburb
ver(a) ver(i)	true, truth	verdict, veracity
vert ver(s)	turn	versatile, revert, reverse, convert

8.
Writing Ability Tests

For some years now, college administrators and teachers have expressed horror and dismay at the declining quality of written English produced by their students. The demand that applicants be tested on their ability to write has been reflected in the increased use of tests of standard written English. In some tests, such as the ACT, English usage tests are part of the basic aptitude battery. ETS doesn't include such tests in the basic SAT, but the Test of Standard Written English (TSWE)—a 30-minute multiple-choice test—is administered with the SAT; the scores are reported separately. A test of your ability to write English is clearly an *achievement* test, of course, but some admissions officers see it as an indication of your *aptitude* for college work—which will include a good deal of work in written English.

You might imagine that the best way to demonstrate your ability to write grammatical English is by *writing*. Not so, say the psychometricians. Over and over, the test-makers of ETS have demonstrated that short-answer tests of writing ability do a better job of predicting grades in English composition classes than essays do. Nowadays, almost all the writing-ability tests are short-answer tests.

SPELLING

Spelling tests are pretty straightforward. Since a printed question can't ask you to spell words, as you would in a spelling bee, you're really asked to *recognize* misspelled words. Actually, this technique is pretty close to the process that occurs when you write. Much of the time, we recognize misspellings in our own writing only when we read it over; we have had so much contact with words that often we get a "feeling" that a word "doesn't look right" The major key to spelling improvement, therefore, is practice.

The most obvious form of spelling test is one that asks you to identify which words are spelled correctly and which aren't. Here is a form commonly found on junior high school and high school level standardized tests:

Directions: Some of the words in the list below are spelled correctly, and some are spelled incorrectly. Blacken space (A) on your answer sheet if the word is spelled *correctly,* and blacken space (B) if it is spelled *incorrectly.*

1. thier	11. adolescence
2. reconnaissance	12. derogetory
3. panacea	13. extraordinary
4. misanthropy	14. formadible
5. frugle	15. libary
6. repugnent	16. inconcievable
7. resuscitate	17. mercenary
8. granular	18. ominous
9. immutible	19. mendacious
10. graphic	20. pecuniary

A variation of this basic recognition form often appears in multiple-choice tests:

Directions: Each group of words includes *one* word that is misspelled. Blacken the space on your answer sheet that corresponds with the letter of the misspelled word.

1. (a) knowledgeable   (d) gullible
   (b) incredable   (e) immutable
   (c) laughable

2. (a) immobility   (d) interrogate
   (b) incorrigible   (e) ludicrous
   (c) abismal

3. (a) misellanious   (d) portentous
   (b) momentous   (e) abeyance
   (c) mitigate

4. (a) supercilious   (d) exhilerate
   (b) exonerate   (e) defoliate
   (c) audible

Remember to read the directions carefully! Often you will be asked to choose the one word that's spelled *correctly*. And often the multiple-choice form will include the option: *none of the above*.

One form of spelling test presents you with the *same* word spelled in a variety of ways. One of the options may be the correct spelling, but be careful. Some tests of this sort can trip you up with lists in which none of the words is correct and the option appears: *none of the above*.

Directions: Choose the correct spelling of each word. If none of the options is correct, blacken space (e) on your answer sheet.

1. (a) occassion   (d) ocasion
   (b) ocassion   (e) none of the above
   (c) occasion

Sometimes you will be presented with a series of sentences. The usual warning applies: read the instructions carefully to find if you are being asked to identify a sentence that contains a spelling error or a sentence that is completely correct.

Directions: Each sentence may contain a spelling error. If there is a sentence in each group that does *not* contain a misspelling, blacken the corresponding space on your answer sheet. If none of the sentences is completely correct, blacken space (e).

(a) In the final analisis, only empirically verifiable data can be cited.
(b) An individual develops concepts only by becoming familiar with specific referants.
(c) When adults attempt to impose mathematical concepts on a child prematurely, the child's learning will be merely verbal.
(d) The first draft of the questionaire was administered to two of the experimental classes.
(e) None of the sentences is correct.

GRAMMAR AND USAGE

On the high school and college levels, tests of grammar and usage are more common than tests of spelling. There are three basic approaches. You may be asked to:
- *recognize* errors;
- *substitute* correct alternatives for faulty items; or
- *identify* the type of error involved.

Here are some ways in which such tests can be presented.

Directions: One of the sentences in each group may be grammatically incorrect. Blacken the space on your answer sheet corresponding to the letter of the incorrect sentence. If *no* sentence is incorrect, blacken space (e).

1. (a) They and we are involved in the program.
   (b) This matter is strictly between you and I.
   (c) Jack is much faster than he.
   (d) If you're looking for the culprit, it is I.
   (e) None of the sentences is incorrect.
2. (a) The use of such drugs is harmful.
   (b) Either of the books is acceptable.
   (c) This kind of matter is not normally discussed.
   (d) Everybody raised their hands.
   (e) None of the sentences is incorrect.

Directions vary. You may be asked to choose the *correct* sentence of a group of mainly incorrect choices. And both types may appear on the same test, so don't assume that one set of directions applies to all the questions in a test or in a section.

Another form of error-recognition focuses on a word or phrase in the context of a passage. This type appears on several tests, including the LSAT:

Directions: The following sentences contain problems in grammar, usage, diction, and idiom. Some sentences are correct. No sentence contains more than one error. If there is an error, it will be underlined and lettered. Select the *one* underlined part that must be changed to make the sentence correct, and blacken the corresponding space on the answer sheet. If there is no error, blacken space E.

1. In the early summer of 1952, <u>before the heat of the campaign,</u>
                                              A
President Truman used to <u>contemplate</u> the problems of the
                              B
<u>General-become-President</u> <u>should Eisenhower</u> win the forthcoming
          C   D
election. <u>No error.</u>
              E

2. The following <u>non-credit courses</u> are not to be considered part of the
                        A
<u>formal college curriculum,</u> which <u>constitute</u> the range of courses from
          B   C
which matriculation credits <u>are to be chosen.</u> <u>No error.</u>
                                    D   E

In the first example, there is no error, although option C presents a style that is not universally accepted; the capitalization in this instance, however, is not incorrect. In looking at example 2, you can see how important it is to learn to read such convoluted sentences (that's how some college bulletins are actually written!). The correct answer is C because the word *constitute* refers to the noun that immediately precedes it: *curriculum*. Since curriculum is singular, the verb should have been *constitutes*.

Substitution questions will ask you to do more than merely recognize errors. The most common form of usage test asks you to substitute from a list an appropriate alternative for a faulty word or phrase.

> **Directions:** In each of the following sentences, a part of the sentence, or the entire sentence, is underlined. For the underlined part, choose the alternative that would produce the most effective and grammatical sentence. If you think that the original is better than any of the alternatives, blacken space A, which repeats the original. Do not choose an alternative that changes the meaning of the sentence.
>
> 1. Both witnesses admitted being involved in and their complicity in the crime.
> (A) being involved in (B) having been involved in
> (C) their involvement (D) their presence at
> (E) involvement in

The grammatical issue here is one of parallel form. The witnesses admitted two things, so the form for both must be the same. You can't change the second phrase because it isn't underlined, so you have to change "being involved in" to a form that is consistent with "their complicity." Option (D) is grammatically correct, but it changes the meaning of the sentence—and the directions warn you against doing this. The forms of (A), (B), and (E) are not parallel with "their complicity." Option (C) is correct.

The form shown on the following pages is becoming standard in the area of usage testing. This is a sample selection from the 1977–1978 *Taking the Act Assessment*.

TEST 1: ENGLISH USAGE

Thor Heyerdahl became famous for a unique sailing expedition, which he later described in *Kon-Tiki*. Having developed a theory that the original Polynesians had sailed or drifted to the South Sea Islands from South America, it then had to be tested. After careful study he
<u>1</u>
built a raft that was as authentic as possible. Using only primitive equipment, he and five other men sailed into the South Seas from Peru, which he judged to be in the same
<u>2</u>
general area as the land of the original Polynesians. As a result, his group and him will
<u>3</u>
long be remembered not only as thorough scientists but also as courageous men.

Heyerdahl's courage was first tested in Ecuador. His search for trees that was large enough for the expeditionary

1. A. NO CHANGE
   B. he set out to test it.
   C. it was decided that it must be tested.
   D. the theory was then to be tested.

2. F. NO CHANGE
   G. Peru, being judged as
   H. Peru, which had been
   J. Peru judged as being

3. A. NO CHANGE
   B. him and his group
   C. his group and himself
   D. he and his group

4. F. NO CHANGE
   G. which would be of sufficient size
   H. of adequate size
   J. of certainly suf-
      ficient size

tension, maintaining that the fish were not
<u>10</u>
dangerous unless a man had already been cut or scratched. One game consisted of luring

sharks within reach, catching them, and then they would yank it onto the raft.
<u>11</u>

Being on the raft, the sharks thrashed about
<u>12</u>
and snapped viciously at the men. Another game was even more dangerous: two men would paddle away on a rubber dinghy until they could catch only an occasional glimpse of
<u>13</u>
the raft; then they would have to paddle violently to return.

The final portion of the voyage was the most

10. F. NO CHANGE
    G. tension. Maintaining
    H. tension. He maintained
    J. tension, because it was maintained

11. A. NO CHANGE
    B. then to yank it and then to
    C. yank them up
    D. and yanking them

12. F. NO CHANGE
    G. At that point,
    H. Once there,
    J. At that time,

13. A. NO CHANGE
    B. (Place after *until*)
    C. (Place after *they*)
    D. OMIT

Andes. There, he and his companions were warned about headhunters and bandits on the trail. Feeling undaunted, they hired a driver
5 .

and jeep from the U.S. Embassy, going on with
6
their dangerous task.

After the raft was done, Heyerdahl made
7

final preparations for the expedition. Even before his crew came aboard,

the courage which Heyerdahl possessed was
8

tested again. As the raft was being towed out of the harbor, it drifted under the stern of a tug. Heyerdahl had to struggle to save it.

Dangers at sea were present, but Heyerdahl
9

and his men did not show fear. Instead they developed games that were actually tests of courage. Although man-eating fish were nearby, the men swam to relieve their

carried rapidly toward the reef, where the waves beat it very bad. Almost miraculously
14

the men survived, only to find theirselves
15

on a deserted island. At last their struggle with the sea had ended. They radioed Rarotonga and set up camp to await rescue.

Thor Heyerdahl's expedition on the Kon-Tiki did not necessarily prove his migration theory, but it did prove that hardy pioneers with courage, determination, and luck could make the same trip, even with very
16

primitive equipment.

B. trail, undaunt-ed, they
C. trail, but they were undaunt-ed, and
D. trail; undaunt-ed they

6. F. NO CHANGE
G. Embassy; and went on with
H. Embassy and proceeded with
J. Embassy, and kept on

7. A. NO CHANGE
B. When the raft was ready,
C. The raft was speedily completed and
D. The raft having been constructed,

8. F. NO CHANGE
G. Heyerdahls' manly courage
H. Heyerdahl's courage
J. the courage of this man

9. A. NO CHANGE
B. (Do not begin new paragraph) At sea. dangers
C. (Begin new paragraph) Dangers, at sea
D. (Begin new paragraph) At sea, dangers

G. mercilessly.
H. very violent.
J. without any mercy.

15. A. NO CHANGE
B. and only found themselves
C. only to find themselves
D. but only found themselves to be

16. F. NO CHANGE
G. could now do the same trip.
H. could do the same,
J. could have ac-complished this the same,

English Usage Answer Key

1. B	5. B	9. D	13. A
2. F	6. H	10. F	.4. G
3. D	7. B	11. D	15. C
4. H	8. H	12. H	16. F

A far less common form of usage test is one that asks you to *identify* the kind of error involved. This type appears usually in advanced tests such as the LSAT.

Directions: Among the sentences in this section are some that are not appropriate in standard written English for the following reasons: *poor diction* (the use of a word that is improper because its meaning does not fit the sentence or because it is not acceptable in standard English usage); *verbosity* (repetitious elements that add nothing to the meaning of the sentence); *faulty grammar* (errors in case, number, parallelism).

No sentence has more than one kind of error. Some sentences may have no errors. On your answer sheet, blacken:

A. if the sentence contains an error in diction;
B. if the sentence is verbose;
C. if the sentence contains faulty grammar;
D. if the sentence contains *none* of these errors.

1. The eyewitness, who had actually seen the accident, presented a detailed account of the events to the jury.
2. Having carefully prepared the papers for the meeting, hopefully it will function smoothly.
3. The regulation of these various and interfering interests forms the principal task of modern legislation.
4. Does the presence of the accused at the scene imprecate him in the crime?

Here's the score:
1. is *verbose:* an eyewitness, by definition, is one who had actually seen something.
2. contains *faulty grammar*: who is the subject of the sentence? Whoever prepared the papers has the right to be hopeful; but the way the sentence reads, the meeting itself is the subject—and it could not have prepared the papers!
3. contains no errors.
4. is an example of *faulty diction*: the word *imprecate* sounds like *implicate*—which *would* have made sense.

One word of caution: don't substitute your *own* definition of errors for those given you in the instructions—a common mistake of test-takers. No matter what *you* think verbosity means, use the definitions given. For example, the LSAT definition of verbosity is "repetitious elements adding nothing to the meaning of the sentence and not justified by any need for special emphasis." Even if *you* think that verbose means wearisome or long-winded or tiresome, this is the *only* definition of verbosity that you should apply on that test. Using the LSAT definition, "the same identical weapon" would be an example of verbosity. This caution underlines the general test-taking rules to:

- read the instructions carefully; and
- avoid confusing your view of what the question *should* have asked with what it *does* ask.

IMPROVING YOUR WRITING ABILITY SKILLS

Writing ability is the least "coachable" of the skills on which you are likely to be tested. Taking a short-term review coaching course, or just reading a chapter like this one, isn't likely to make significant changes in the writing habits you have built up over a lifetime. But that doesn't mean that you can't improve. If you have trouble with spelling, grammar, or style, you should begin a long-range, systematic program of retraining. If it's possible, find a long-range school program of remediation. If this isn't possible, embark on such a program on your own. Your task is to build up a new *modus operandi* to replace the one you've developed over the years. (Some suggestions are offered below.)

On the other hand, if your grasp of spelling, grammar, and usage is fundamentally sound, but you want some fast review tips, some specific rules are offered in the pages that follow.

SPELLING

A long-range program makes sense only if you stick to it faithfully. It's easy to skip a day or two—and this makes it easier to *continue* to skip. If you are serious about improving, following your program regularly.

In a notebook, keep a list of words you misspell. Include every word you misspell during the day. Review your list daily. Maintaining a list is time-consuming, but you're trying to break habits that took a long time to develop.

Use the dictionary. Guessing at the spelling of a word you don't know saves a good deal of time. Besides, it adds a certain spontaneity and sporting quality to academic pursuits. But if you want to build up a spelling inventory, you'll have to make a *habit* of referring to the dictionary. (When you're not sure of the spelling, you'll have enough of the gambling element just finding the word you want!) If a dictionary is available, use it as soon as you realize that you aren't *positive* how a word is spelled. Otherwise, check the spelling as you review your daily additions to your list. The dictionary will also show you words that appear alphabetically above and below the word you want; you may see connections in terms of prefixes or roots.

Spell by syllables. Many of the words you'll have trouble with have several syllables. Dividing a word into syllables creates a number of shorter words, some of which you may already know how to spell. Some of these shorter words may have meanings of their own (such as post-war, or auto-mobile); some may not.

117

Pronounce words correctly. If you consistently mispronounce a word, it's hard to spell it correctly. For example:

if you say	*it's hard to spell*
athaletic	athletic
extrawdinary	extraordinary
liberry	library
prespiration	perspiration
probly or probally	probably
supprise	surprise
artic	arctic
anticlimatic	anticlimactic
beneffishary	beneficiary
realator	realtor
Febuary	February

Relate words to simpler words from which they come. Many words are composites. If you can identify the root words, the spelling is often much more obvious.

Learn some basic rules. Some words are unique; they don't follow any rules. But a large number of words fall into categories. If you learn and remember a handful of basic rules, you should be able to figure out the spelling of a large number of words. Most rules have exceptions, but if you apply the rules when in doubt, the odds are in your favor.

- *When the sound is* ee, *the spelling is* ie *(think* pie*), except after* c.
  examples: belief, achieve, brief, pierce, reprieve
  after *c*: receive, perceive, ceiling
  exceptions: weird, either, seize
- *When the sound is not* ee, *the spelling is* ei.
  examples: weigh, height, deign, foreign, veil, freight
  exceptions: friend, sieve, handkerchief
- *The root word remains the same when the following prefixes are added:* dis-, il-, im-, in-, mis-, over-, re-, *and* un-.
  examples:
  dis + engage = disengage
  il + legal = illegal
  im + possible = impossible
  in + sensitive = insensitive
  mis + understood = misunderstood
  over + eat = overeat
  re + move = remove
  un + clear = unclear
- *The root word remains the same when the following suffixes are added:* -ness *and* -ly.
  examples:
  general + ly = generally
  brutal + ly = brutally

open + ness = openness
exception: If word ends in *y*, change the *y* to *i* before you add a suffix.
greedy + ness = greediness
plenty + ful = plentiful
heavy + ness = heaviness

- *Drop the final* e *before a suffix beginning with a vowel.*
examples:
take + ing = taking
move + able = movable
exception: If the *e* is preceded by a *c* or a *g* with a soft sound, keep the final *e*.
change + able = changeable
knowledge + able = knowledgeable
notice + able = noticeable
- *Keep the final* e *if the suffix begins with a consonant.*
examples:
hope + ful = hopeful
care + less = careless

GRAMMAR AND USAGE

As with spelling, a program of improvement in grammar and usage must be long-range. If your general ability in the field is sound but you need some review, here are some tips and hints.

Three areas of grammar give many test-takers particular trouble: *case, number,* and *modifiers*. In each area, the problem involves having one part of a sentence or a paragraph agree with another part.

Case has to do with pronouns. You'll remember that nouns are words that describe people, places, or things. You use pronouns such as *he, she,* or *it* instead of repeating the noun each time. The pronoun has to agree with the noun it replaces. There are three cases: nominative, objective, and possessive. Here are the two with which many test-takers have trouble.

Nominative Case
Subject: the person, place, or thing that *is* doing or being

Objective Case
Object: the person, place, or thing *for which* something is done or *to which* something is done

He walks. *It* is big.
I
you
he, she, it
we
you
they

Give it to *her*. Hit *it*.
me
you
him, her, it
us
you
them

I gave it to *him*.
He gave it to *me*.

The basic tip is that when you're unsure of the case, try: (1) *leaving out the parts of the sentence that are irrelevant*, or (2) *adding the parts that were understood but left out.* Here's how it works:

Leave out. Mentally, leave out all the pronouns *except* the one with which you're having trouble. Putting the sentence together with just the basic elements will usually give you the answer, because you can see the relationship between the pronoun and the verb with which it must agree.

Jack gave (he, him) and (I, me) the information we needed.

Now let's leave out the extraneous pronoun and concentrate on one at a time:

Jack gave *him*   ...   the information. . .
Jack gave   ...   *me* the information. . .

Put them together:

Jack gave him and me the information we needed.

Similarly,

> *The gift is for* you and *them.*
> *Let's go with* Elaine and *her.*
> You and *I have to work* this through.

This technique works no matter how many nouns or pronouns are involved.

> Elaine and Laurie and Karen and Norma and Brian and Debbie and Maddy and *I went to the party.*

Add the unstated parts. The statement, "Hit it" doesn't seem to have a subject. But somebody has to do the hitting. The sentence is really, "[You] hit it." Often parts of a sentence are understood but are not *stated*; this is why you may often have trouble with case. Mentally add the unstated portion, and the proper pronoun will usually become clear—because it must agree with the verb.

My father is not as tall as (I, me).

add: My father is not as tall as I [am].

Similarly:

> Phyllis played a better game than he [did].
> It was I [who went].
> I like Sam better than [I like] him.

Number refers to the fact that verbs have to agree with their subjects in number. As with case, most people have no trouble with the simple statements like:

the *child asks*	the *children ask*
he does	*they do*
she doesn't	*they don't*

(Some people have trouble even here. A simple rule: Always use *doesn't* (not *don't*) after *he, she* or it.)

As with case, the basic tip is (1) *leave out irrelevant parts,* or (2) *add unstated parts.*

Leave out. You can see relationships more clearly by leaving out the sections of the sentence that confuse the relationship between subject and verb.

One was late.

The presence of additional words doesn't change this relationship:

> One [of the teachers who normally drive to school] was late [because heavy snow blocked the road].

Similarly:

> One set [of directions] applies [to the whole test].
>
> All [of the corporation officers who handled the accounts] were responsible.

Often words like *one* are built into a word or phrase; but it's still *one*. Leave out the rest of the word to see which verb form to use.

> [Every]one [of you] belongs here.
>
> [Any]one can do it if he or she wants.

As with case, don't be thrown if strings of nouns or pronouns are joined together. Singular subjects joined together with *or* or *nor* are still singular.

> *Either* Sally or Sam [one of them] *is coming.*
>
> *Neither* the major nor the captain *knows what he is doing.*

Add the unstated parts. Words like *either, neither,* and *each* have an unstated *one* built in. By adding the *one* mentally, you can see more clearly whether the verb and any pronouns are singular or plural.

> Either [one] of you can take his (or her) seat.
>
> Each [one] of these books is worth reading.
>
> Neither [one] of these cards belongs here.

Modifiers can be incredibly complicated if you get into some of the technicalities. But you can often *use* modifiers correctly without knowing whether they are adverbs or adjectives, superlatives or comparatives. Normally, most test graders don't care if you know the rules as long as you *use* modifiers correctly. Here are the two most common errors in the use of modifiers:

• *Dangling modifiers* are phrases that don't relate to the word that they're supposed to modify. That first question on the ACT English Usage Test was focused on a dangling modifier.

> Having developed a theory that. . . , it then had to be tested.

Here's the basic tip: when you come across any sentence that begins with a modifying phrase, ask *Who*? That same person or thing has to be the subject of the *other* phrase or clause. Let's see how it works.

> Having developed a theory . . . [Who did? Why, Heyerdahl, of course], he set out to test it.

• *Misplaced modifiers* are words, phrases, or clauses that are used in such a way as to suggest that they're modifying the wrong word or phrase. For example:

> Is there a student in the auditorium with a brown jacket?
>
> [Have *you* ever seen an auditorium with a brown jacket?]
>
> I borrowed a ladder from a neighbor that's 30 feet long.
>
> [Now, *that's* a long neighbor.]
>
> I caught a trout with my new fishing gear which I fried over a wood fire.
>
> [Have you ever tried fried fishing gear?]

She wore a pair of diamond clips in her ears which she brought from New York.
[She probably would have felt naked without her ears.]

The basic tip: Rearrange the sentence so that the modifier *is as close as possible* to the word or phrase it modifies. For example:

Is there a student with a brown jacket in the auditorium?
I borrowed a 30-foot ladder from a neighbor.
With my new fishing gear, I caught a trout which I fried over a wood fire.
In her ears, she wore a pair of diamond clips which she brought from New York.

This very short review is designed to help you brush up on usage, and to provide tips and reminders. It isn't a course in English usage, or a remedial grammar course. If you have real problems with standard English usage, you'll need help. Some individuals might have the motivation and the persistence to undertake a self-improvement program with a good grammar or program designed for self-instruction. If you're not one of them, you probably need the discipline of a formal remedial course. You might check at your high school or college to see if such a course is offered, or if the counselors know of such a course elsewhere.

9.
Numerical Ability Tests

Originally, numerical ability tests tended to contain straight math questions—mainly in arithmetic and algebra, with some geometry thrown in from time to time. The standardized achievement tests in math still consist mostly of such questions. But over the years, the scholastic ability or aptitude tests—the tests that are designed to predict—have tended to move away from the straight manipulation of numbers and formulas to deal with the *logic* of problem solving. In other words, questions call on you to manipulate the information in order to force an answer, rather than to memorize or apply a formula or a technique that you've learned. There is also an increasing emphasis on the "property" of numbers—the way numbers fit into a system. In fact, some aptitude tests, such as the SAT, will often *give* you the formulas you need because they're more interested in how you handle the problem than in whether you remember the formula. In any event, on most of the aptitude tests the math won't go beyond beginning algebra or first-year geometry. (See the description of the SAT in Chapter 6.)

These two changes have had some interesting effects. For one thing, because the math sections of these tests have moved from straight computation to reasoning, they seem to be measuring something very similar to whatever it is the verbal tests measure; the correlations are higher than they used to be. This has caused a number of critics to ask why college or graduate school applicants should have to take the math portions of the tests, especially if they have no intention of being caught dead near the engineering or science or accounting departments.

In addition, because of the current stress on reasoning and basic principles rather than on manipulation, some of the symbolic systems have changed. A lot of test-takers are thrown into a panic when confronted with math problems in which quantities are represented not by numerals, but by letters or other symbols. Relax; the basic principles don't change. And if you know how to handle a situation with numbers, you should be able to handle it with any symbols the test-makers choose to toss at you.

Here are some of the basic strategies for coping with math tests, or tests of "numerical ability" or "quantitative reasoning," or whatever else they may be called.

Know what's being asked of you. Because numerical problems often have so many parts, it's very easy to lose focus of what you've been asked to do. Are you to find the area of a segment? The percentage of profit in a sale transaction? Or the number of cents in the cost of a screwdriver? In each case, you may be manipulating numbers and fragments that aren't expressed in the terms that you want (area, percent, cents); they may have to be converted or manipulated to get what you want.

If you have trouble keeping focused on your purpose, write at the top of your scrap paper the key words (*cents, dollars, miles, percentages,* etc.) in which your answer must be expressed. For example:

> A carpenter uses an average of 10 nails a minute. How many dozen nails will he have used at the end of 3 hours?
> (a) 125   (b) 150   (c) 900   (d) 1200   (e) 1800

The calculations in this problem are relatively simple. The carpenter would use 600 nails an hour (that first conversion, from minutes to hours, wasn't too difficult: 10 nails a minutes × 60 minutes). At the end of 3 hours, he would have used 1800 nails; since 1800 is among the options, you proceed to blacken the space for option (e)—and lose credit for the problem on which you've already invested all this time! The question asked how many *dozen* nails he would have used (1800 nails divided by 12 = 150 dozen nails). If you had circled the key terms as you read the problem, or if you had written *dozens of nails* on your scrap paper, you wouldn't be as likely to make this mistake.

Speaking of scrap paper—on a standardized test nobody will examine your scrap paper, so use it only as necessary. If you *can* calculate more quickly in your head, do so. Only the correct answer counts, and you don't have to show your work, as you do in many classroom tests.

Note other key terms, words, and data that are given you. Does the question provide such information as the fact that a triangle is isosceles or that a "dressed" 1 × 12 plank is actually ¾" by 11½"? If so, assume that such information is given you *for a purpose.* Part of your task is to figure out *why* you were given these tidbits. Unless you're alert, it's easy under pressure to miss such information, or to ignore it once you're involved in the calculations. Even in the simple question above, it would be possible to miss the fact that the rate of nailing was given in *minutes,* but that the total is asked in terms of *hours.* If the key terms are short (and if this is the kind of test in which you're permitted to write on the question paper), underline or circle them. Otherwise note them on your scrap paper.

Convert the information into forms that are meaningful for you. This means, among other possibilities, that you might:

Express a problem in equation form:
If 5% of the widgets produced in a factory are rejected because of damage, how many widgets must be produced in order to yield 874 salable ones?
(a) 437   (b) 920   (c) 930   (d) 1,037   (e) 1,437

If you let x represent the total number of widgets that has to be produced, then 874 is 95% of x. In simple equation form, this becomes: $.95x = 874$. $\frac{874}{.95} = 920$

To avoid thinking in abstractions, substitute simple numbers for symbols.
Typist A completes x letters a day. Typist B produces 10 letters a day more than typist A. Typist C produces twice as many letters a day as typist B. How many more letters does C produce than A?
(a) $x + 10$ (b) $x + 20$ (c) $2x$ (d) $2x + 10$ (e) $2x + 20$

If you substitute a small number like 5 for x, then you know that: A produces 5 letters; B produces 15 letters; C types 30. For each option in the question, by substituting the number 5 for x, you find that (a) would yield 15, (b) would yield 25, (c) would yield 10, (d) would yield 20, and (e) would yield 30. So (e) tells you how many letters typist C types. But if you've noted the key words, you'll be aware *that's not what you were asked to find*! You're to find how many *more* letters C typed than were typed by A. Again, using that substitute number, you can come up with 25—and option (b).

It was noted that a current trend is to test you for the properties of numbers, rather than mere rote manipulation. One way a test will accomplish this is by using non-numerical symbols—either with or without numbers—so that you're dealing with abstractions. For example:

If $X > Z$, which of the following must be true?
(a) $X > 2Z$ (b) $X > Z + 2$ (c) $X > \frac{X+Z}{2}$ (d) $X > Y$ (e) $\frac{X}{2} > Z$

If you have trouble with this kind of question, try substituting simple numerals. Since the difference between X and Z *may* be very small [see option (b)], your sample numerals should be small and close to each other—perhaps 1 and 2. Even if you can figure this out without substitutions, it's a good idea to check your answer out with numeral substitutions.

Reconstruct a formula you have forgotten by substituting small numbers. Often you perform some manipulations intuitively or by rote, without consciously applying an appropriate formula. When the situation is changed somewhat, you may have trouble with the specifics unless you can reconstruct the formula. This is often the case with such general rules as those having to do with rate, time, and distance. If you can't think of the formula offhand, think of the problem in terms of simple numbers. For example, even if you can't remember that *rate* equals *distance* divided by *time* $(r = \frac{d}{t})$, you should be able to figure out that if you travel 100 miles in 2 hours, you're traveling at the rate of 50 miles an hour. Simply substitute the appropriate terms for the numbers.

Draw a diagram with all parts labeled accurately. The diagram itself may suggest a procedure for dealing with the problem.

How many square feet are in a garden which is twice as long as it is wide if the fence around it is 600 feet long?

(a) 4,000   (b) 10,000   (c) 20,000   (d) 36,000   (e) 72,000

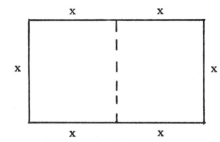

There are six sections of equal length. Since the fence is 600 feet, each section must be 100 feet; the garden must be 100 feet by 200 feet, and the area is 20,000 square feet.

Try working backwards from the options. In some kinds of problems, you might save time by simply substituting each option for the unknown and finding the correct one by trial-and-error.

John is one-third his father's age. In 12 years, he will be half his father's age. How old is John now?

(a) 10 years   (b) 12 years   (c) 15 years   (d) 18 years

Simply start substituting each option.

(a) If John is 10, his father must be 30. In 12 years, John will be 22, his father will be 42; 22 is not half of 42.

(b) If John is 12, his father must be 36. In 12 years, John will be 24, his father 48. This works out to the specifications of the problem, so (b) must be correct.

Here are two sample problems from the 1978 *Taking the ACT Assessment*;* as they are presented, the most appropriate way of dealing with them is to work backwards from options.

The following multiplication scheme uses symbols other than the usual numerals. △ corresponds to which base-10 numeral?

$$\triangle \times \ominus = \ominus$$

$$\ominus \times \triangle = \ominus$$

$$\triangle \times \triangle = \triangle$$

A. 0
B. 1
C. 2

D. 5
E. 10

(answer: B)

What set of values for x and y (x,y) satisfy the equations below:
$$3y = x + 4$$
$$6x + 2y = 16$$

A. $(-2, 2)$
B. $(2, -2)$
C. $(-2, -2)$

D. $(2, 2)$
E. None of the above

(answer: D)

Ask some additional questions. Here are some of the questions you might ask:

Are there new ways of using the data given you that you had not already used? Are there clues that suggest familiar formulas or methods? Are options presented in forms that suggest methods of approach? For example, are options expressed in degrees, or in terms of π, or in phrases that suggest approaches (like "the sum of the squares of the sides")? Be careful, though—some may be designed as "attractive distractors." Use clues in options only as possibilities.

Does the problem itself suggest similar problems you have worked on in class?

Does changing or adding an element make the problem clearer? In geometry, for example, it's often advisable to add auxiliary lines to the diagram presented in the problem. If the question asks about *a* triangle, would the problem be more clear if you thought of a *right* triangle, or an *equilateral* triangle? (Be careful here that your solution doesn't apply *only* to right or equilateral triangles.)

Are you missing data that you need to solve the problem? Is there a way for you to figure out the missing information from what you have been given?

Work out your calculations. Once you have decided on your procedures, work your calculations carefully and step by step. Many low scorers actually work out a good plan, and then forget it when they begin to work their calculations. It might be a good idea to note briefly, in order, what steps you must take and then check each one off as you perform it. Some practical hints on calculation:

• Focus again on what it is you have to do and be sure your plan will help you arrive at an answer.

• If possible, estimate a figure mentally, so that you can judge if your calculations are on the track.

• Be sure that all your units are converted into the same *system* (metric or fahrenheit, for example) or the same *unit* (cents, yards, or minutes). Be especially sure that when you have finished, the answer is in terms of units in the options.

• Proceed systematically, step by step. If a thought occurs to you about a step that you have to take later, note it or remember it, but don't jump from operation to operation. (However, work as quickly as you can without sacrificing accuracy.)

Check your work. It's not the smartest thing in the world to spend a good deal of time and effort in calculating an answer and then lose the credit because you didn't check it out. Checking may involve reviewing your calculations, but it's much more than that. It means ascertaining if your answer makes sense in terms of the thrust of the question.

• How close is your answer to your preliminary estimate? If it's way off, why? Was your estimate wrong, or did you make a mistake in procedure or in calculation?

• Is the answer reasonable in terms of the nature of the question? If you're trying to figure out the cost of individual toothbrushes when a box costs $36, then obviously an answer of $142 isn't very reasonable.

• Will substitutions hold up? Substituting small numbers can often help in checking an answer, just as it can in figuring out a procedure or a formula. If the answer is in algebraic terms or in a formula, will it work out if you substitute numbers for the symbols?

• Did you leave out any of the data given you in the question? Could the information you ignored have been useful in solving the problem or in answering the question?

• If your answer doesn't match any of the options, could the mistake be as obvious as adding or leaving out a zero somewhere in the calculations? Or could it be in the decimals? Did you skip a step?

• Are the units consistent all the way through? Did you convert dollars and cents, or inches and feet, or minutes and hours, so that you're calculating with comparable units?

• Is a recalculation called for? In this case, don't just repeat. And *don't* look at your old calculations; you may end up overlooking or repeating a mistake. Calculate in a different way, perhaps using decimals for fractions, adding from bottom to top, reversing multiplier and multiplicand.

• Is your answer really the answer to the question in terms of what you were asked to find?

NUMERICAL SERIES

Basically the same kind of thinking is involved in numerical series problems as with those verbal analogies in Chapter 7, but the symbols used here are numerals rather than words. Also, most number analogies are not presented in the common form that you've seen: A is to B as C is to ____?____; you need more information to figure out the relationships between numbers, which, unlike words, are rather neutral in their impact. Therefore, the numerical analogy is usually presented as a series of numbers with one item (usually, but not always, the last one) missing. Here is a fairly standard way in which such items appear:

2   4   8   16   32   _____
(a) 28   (b) 46   (c) 48   (d) 64   (e) none of these

Just glancing at this series should show you that the numbers keep getting bigger, and that the differences between them also increase. It shouldn't have taken you long to realize that the numbers keep doubling. Obviously, the number series you can expect to find on tests will be more complicated than this. But if you don't panic and do work systematically, you should be able to work out the relationships.

Here are some of the steps.

• *Play your first hunch.* Often you can see the relationship by just examining the series and getting a "feel" for the way the numbers change. As you glanced at the series above, you might quickly have seen the doubling without working out specifics. But don't let it go at hunch-playing; *test your hunch all the way through the series.*

• *Identify the major kinds of changes.* Do the numbers keep getting larger all the way through the series? Smaller? Alternatively larger and smaller?

• *Write out the differences between the numbers.* If you're permitted to write on the question sheet, do it under the space; otherwise write out the whole series on scrap paper and do your calculations on it. Often the relationship sticks out like a sore thumb when you do this.

5   12   19   26   _____   40
+7   +7   +7   +7(?)
(a) 33   (b) 37   (c) 47   (d) 54   (e) none of these

Even if the relationship is a little more complicated, writing out the differences will help give you a key. Try this one:

2   6   4   12   10   30   28   _____
(a) 26   (b) 38   (c) 84   (d) 50   (e) none of these

Now let's work it out with the differences.

2   6   4   12   10   30   28   _____
+4   −2   +8   −2   +20   −2

As you look at the pattern, it becomes clear that the only regularity here is the alternate −2. So let's keep that relationship and go back to refigure the others. *Those numbers increase, but the differences don't seem to be simple additions. There are several possibilities, but one easy one to check is that of multiplication.*

2   6   4   12   10   30   28   _____
×3   −2   ×3   −2   ×3   −2

That pattern just jumped out of the problem; it's regular and predictable. The next operation must be to multiply 28 × 3 and mark option (c) as your answer.

Often the *differences* show the pattern much more clearly than trial-and-error manipulation of the numbers themselves. Try this one:

2 5 11 23 47 95 _____

The relationships here would take a good deal of manipulation to find (they involve *multiplication by two* and *addition of one*). But if you write the differences, a much clearer pattern emerges:

```
2    5    11    23    47    95    _____
  +3   +6   +12   +24   +48
```

Even if you hadn't figured out the relationship of (×2, +1), you see that the differences keep doubling; so the next number must be 96 more than the previous one—or 191.

• *Consider the differences as part of the series.* Sometimes the differences themselves are actually part of the calculation in the series—and the *differences of the differences* may provide the key.

```
2    3    8    19    38    67    _____
 +1    +5   +11   +19   +29      +41(?)
   +4    +6    +8   +10   +12(?)
```

After you've spent some time on the differences without getting anywhere, you might try to carry the process one step further. The *differences of the differences* show a pattern of increasing by 2. Inserting the two missing differences, you find that you must add 41 to the last number of the series, to arrive at an answer of 108.

• *Look for alternative groupings.* Especially if the numbers don't increase or decrease in a consistent pattern, you may have to look for alternative patterns, in which numbers may be grouped in pairs or triplets. In such cases, you have two tasks:

(1) to find the relationship *within* each group;
(2) to find the relationship *between* the groups.

Here's one that will defy analysis, unless you play around with the possibility of alternative groupings:

```
3   5   7   9   11   13    27   29   31   _____
 +2  +2  +2  +2   +2   +14   +2   +2
```

That +14 breaks up what seemed to be a very simple and obvious pattern. This makes it clear that the relationship is not one of straight addition. If we examine the series again, we look for different kinds of groupings, starting at the point of:

```
3   5   7      9   11   13      27   29   31
 +2  +2         +2   +2          +2   +2
```

So far, so good. We've located the pattern *within* each group. Now let's start with the first number in each group. After a few false starts, you might come up with:

$$\overbrace{}^{\times 3}\quad\overbrace{}^{\times 3}$$
$$3 \quad 5 \quad 7 \quad 9 \quad 11 \quad 13 \quad 27 \quad 29 \quad 31$$

The pattern, then, is the division of the series into three groups; the first number of each group is three times the first number of the preceding group; and within each group, the numbers increase regularly by the addition of 2.

• *Try alternative relationships.* Start with the simpler relationships—addition and multiplication for increasing numbers, subtraction and division for decreasing ones. If these don't show a pattern, keep cool. For example, you might consider squares of the numbers, or square roots:

$$2^2 \qquad 4^2 \qquad 16^2 \qquad 256^2$$
$$2 \quad 4 \quad\; 4 \quad 6 \quad\; 16 \quad 18 \quad\; 256 \quad\;\; 258$$
$$+2 \qquad +2 \qquad +2 \qquad\;\; +2$$

TESTS OF GRAPH AND CHART READING

Many math tests have sections that deal with your ability to read charts and graphs. Technically, these aren't math questions, but they do deal with comparative quantities. On some tests, they're in a separate section, but the ETS aptitude tests usually include them in the math sections.

Tests of this type usually deal with several abilities and skills:

• Your ability to *read and translate* the graph or chart has to do with how well you recognize the kind of information being presented, and whether you can *decode* it. In other words, can you figure out what the graph is about, and can you pinpoint a particular piece of information from it?

• Your ability to *interpret* the graph is the ease with which you can see relationships between different sets of data so as to explain one in terms of the other. It has a good deal to do with *how* and *why*.

• Your ability to *draw conclusions* is really a combination of abilities, such as your ability to *interpolate* and *extrapolate* and your ability to draw inferences from given information and to figure out probabilities.

There are many kinds of tables, charts, and graphs, and there's no way for you to anticipate and prepare for any particular kind. For example, graphs can be circle graphs, bar graphs, square or space graphs, picture graphs, and line graphs. Each is designed to present data in a somewhat different way and for a somewhat different purpose. Line graphs, for instance, are designed to show changes, whereas bar graphs are used to compare similar sets of data; circle graphs show proportions or parts of a total.

The most common form of graph on tests is probably the line graph, but the same general *kind* of analysis and thinking is involved in most graph questions.

Let's use as a model the following line graph:

Worldwide Military Expenditures, 1961–1973

Billions of dollars

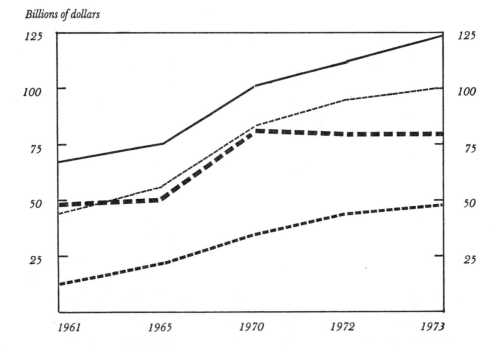

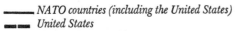 NATO countries (including the United States)
United States
Warsaw Pact countries
Other

Source: U.S. Bureau of the Census

1. Military spending by NATO countries in 1973 totaled approximately how many billions of dollars?
(a) 56   (b) 75   (c) 100   (d) 105   (e) 120

2. In what year did United States military spending reach its peak?
(a) 1961   (b) 1965   (c) 1968   (d) 1970   (e) 1973

3. The spending of the Warsaw Pact nations surpassed that of the United States
(a) before 1961   (b) in 1961   (c) in 1963   (d) in 1965   (e) in 1970.

4. What is the percentage increase of NATO military spending from 1965 to 1970?
(a) 0%   (b) 10%   (c) 20%   (d) 40%   (e) 70%

5. Approximately what percentage of worldwide military spending was done by NATO countries in 1970?
(a) 10%   (b) 20%   (c) 30%   (d) 40%   (e) 50%

6. Based on information in the graph, which one of the following statements is *incorrect*?
(a) United States military spending remained constant between 1970 and 1973.
(b) The proportionate increase in military spending between 1961 and 1973 was greatest for countries other than those in NATO or the Warsaw Pact.
(c) For all nations, the greatest spurt in military spending occurred between 1965 and 1970.
(d) United States military spending declined between the years 1961 and 1965.
(e) The United States, throughout the period, accounted for more than half the military spending of NATO.

7. Of the following, which is the best estimate of U.S. military spending in 1968, in billions of dollars?
(a) 48   (b) 50   (c) 65   (d) 78   (e) 90

The first three of these questions focus on straight graph reading, as does the sixth, although the form is somewhat different. The fourth involves some computation based on the figures you read. The fifth also involves computation, but it's more complicated: you have to read and add the totals for all groups *except the United States* (the key told you that the NATO countries *include* the U.S.), then calculate the percentage (it's 50%, by the way). Question seven calls on you to interpolate, or to calculate a figure between the two figures that you can read off the graph.

Here are some hints on dealing with chart and graph questions:
Know what the graph or chart shows. In most such tests, you will see a label for each chart or graph. But if there is none, you must ask yourself what the graph is showing; in other words, what would be the title or label?

On graphs, identify the axes. What are the variables? What does the vertical (or *y* axis) show? What does the horizontal (or *x* axis) show? What seems to be the basic relationship between them?

What are the graph scales? It's very easy to misinterpret graphs on the basis of just visual comparisons. For example, the following graphs show exactly the same relationships between the two sets of information. The angles have been changed by the spacing of the vertical and horizontal scales. Moreover, you might have noticed that in Graph C, each demarcation represents *three* units, not one. Be sure to check on the scale; don't assume that they are equal on the two axes or that they are in single—or even in even—intervals.

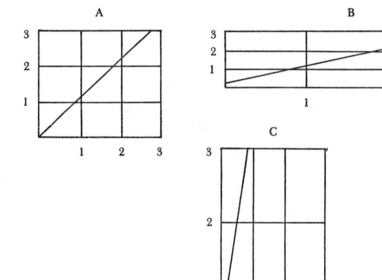

Use a graph to find data rather than to estimate from appearance alone. Funny things can be done with statistics, and even funnier things with graphs. (You must have heard the old saw that statistics don't lie—but statisticians do.) Let's see how easy it is to jump to a mistaken conclusion based on the appearance of a graph.

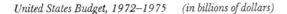

United States Budget, 1972–1975   *(in billions of dollars)*

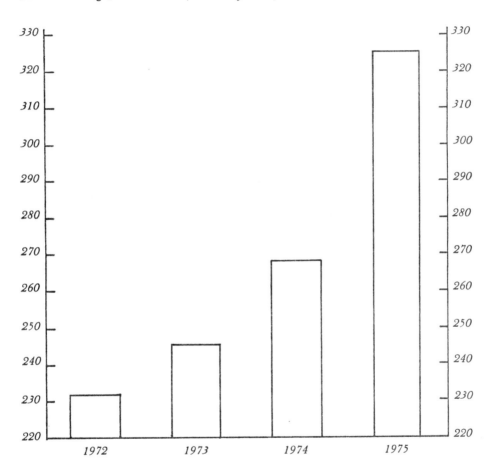

135

In 1973 the United States budget increased over 1972 by (a) less than 10%
(b) 25%   (c) 50%   (d) 100%   (e) 120%.

If you judged only by appearances, you might choose either (d) or (e) on the
ground that the bar for 1973 is more than twice as high as the bar for 1972. This
would be true *if* the dollar figures began at zero. But the axis showing the budget
outlay begins at $220 billion; so the actual increase between 1972 and 1973 was
less than 10%. Don't jump to conclusions based on the looks of a graph. Check
carefully against the scales, using a ruler or a piece of paper as a guide. Sometimes
you might have to interpolate or extrapolate if the specific information is not given
directly. But even in such a case, check against the scale and use the scale figures.

Be aware of the differences between graphs. That doesn't just mean the difference between a bar graph, a line graph, and a circle graph (or "pie-shaped"
graph in which wedges of different sizes indicate how a whole is distributed).
Sometimes one graph may *look* something like another, but *show* something very
different. For example, the graph below may look at first like the line graphs about
which we've been talking.

Research and Development Funds, by Performance Sector and Source: 1960–1976

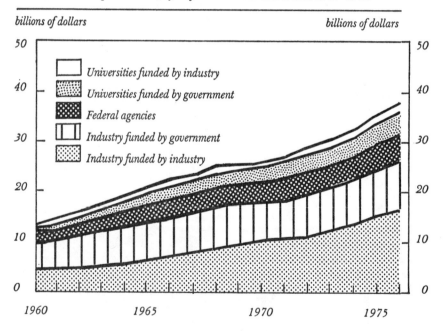

Chart prepared by U.S. Bureau of the Census. Data from U.S. National Science Foundation.

136

Of the institutions conducting research, which single group received the most money?   (a) universities funded by industry   (b) universities funded by the government   (c) industry funded by industry   (d) industry funded by the government   (e) federal agencies

If your first reaction is to look at the top line of this graph to find how much money was received by universities funded by industry, then you're thinking of the straight-line graph with a common base. But the fact that the line for this group ends at $35 billion does *not* mean that this group *received* $35 billion. This kind of graph is built on cumulative or additive figures. The actual amount received by universities funded by industry is just the *portion* of the $35 billion (the total amount that *all* the groups received) that's included between the top and bottom line for the group. The group in this graph that received the most money was industry funded by industry, because it has the *widest* band.

The use of graph and table items in standardized tests is growing because a good deal of information can be given in a small space—and the test-maker can measure a lot of different abilities based on this information. If you're not thoroughly familiar with graph and table reading, some library practice won't hurt.

10.
The Essay Examination

A lot of critics have attacked the objective test that has now become the best-known form of mass test. About twenty years ago, when standardized testing had not yet become as widespread as it is today, President A. Whitney Griswold of Yale said that "A few teachers still prefer written essays to intellectual bingo games that can be scored by electricity." And in his 1962 book, *The Tyranny of Testing*, Queens College mathematics professor Banesh Hoffman fired a blistering attack on the use of standardized tests. He demonstrated that intelligent adults who actually *teach* the subject on which a test is based are likely to pick "wrong" answers. "Multiple-choice tests," he told an interviewer in 1975, "penalize the deep student, dampen creativity, foster intellectual dishonesty, and undermine the very foundations of education." Hoffman complains that standardized tests don't show the mental processes behind the choice of answers. He is bitter about the control of education by "technicians of evaluation" and argues that teachers must be most concerned, not with right or wrong answers, but with the reasoning behind them. The only way to discover this reasoning, contends Hoffman, is with such tests as the essay, which, he argues, are better than short-answer tests in measuring "real" understanding. But are they?

Essay tests, theoretically, are designed to measure abilities like creativity or organization of ideas, that are not easily measured in short-answer tests. If anything, though, the essay questions that appear on most classroom examinations tend to be even more poorly designed than the short-answer tests. For one thing, most of them violate the basic rule of normative testing: that people can be compared with each other only if they are all given the same or comparable "standard tasks."

The problem in many (if not most) essay tests is that the samples are not comparable—for a variety of reasons. They aren't comparable if the questions are worded so ambiguously that several individuals can legitimately interpret the question in various ways. For example, the most commonly used word on essay examinations is probably *discuss*, which can be interpreted to mean: *trace, outline, describe, compare, list, explain, evaluate, defend, criticize, summarize,* or *tell all you know about* a subject.

The samples aren't uniform or standard or comparable if the question can invite responses that the grader doesn't think are relevant to the question. But most essay questions are so unrestricted that there is no effective guidance for the test-taker. For instance, "give examples" may mean to one test-taker that he is expected to present two examples; another may interpret the instruction as a demand to cite as many examples as he can think of. Neither one knows how many the examiner is prepared to accept for full credit, unless the question itself makes it clear. In fact, the examiner may not have considered this issue when he wrote the question! In all too many cases, the essay test-maker does not have a clearly defined set of standards by which to evaluate the responses.

It has always been known that the grading of essay tests is subjective. But a study of test grading shortly after the turn of the century made it clear just *how* subjective it was. In 1912, Daniel Starch and Edward Elliot questioned the growing use of grades to indicate student proficiency. They reproduced two English examination papers and sent them to 200 high schools to be graded by experienced English teachers; 142 papers were graded and returned. One paper received grades that ranged from 50 to 98, and the other from 64 to 99.

The study caused quite a stir among teachers. Some admitted that there was room for a spread in a subject like English, and they dared Starch and Elliot to repeat their study in an "objective" subject like math. So Starch and Elliot sent a geometry paper to 138 geometry teachers. The range in grades was even greater than in English! Grades were distributed between 28 and 95—and the distribution followed the normal curve. Some teachers deducted points for wrong answers, some for sloppiness, or spelling errors, or form, or procedure.

What was particularly noteworthy about the studies was the fact that the "probable error"—or chance alone—would account for only a 7-point difference among the grades given a single paper, based on the "average" grade of 85. But the math paper (given 80% by the test-taker's own teacher) was given failing grades by 15% of the teachers and grades of over 90 by 12%.

As if it weren't enough to show differences *between* teachers, a number of studies were concerned with the grades given a paper by the *same* teacher. It was demonstrated, over and over again, that the same teacher, given a paper at different times, would give it markedly different grades (the pun is unintentional).

Such demonstrations helped promote the growing popularity of the objective short-answer test. Of course, the major difference is not that the essay test is more subjective than the short-answer test. The major difference is that the essay's subjectivity is more obvious because it shows up in the grading, while the "objective" test has its subjectivity hidden in the choice of questions and the range of options in the answers provided. The objective test gives the appearance of objectivity by removing the element of teacher whim from the grading process. And it was the increasing popularity of the objective test that made possible the growth of the standardized test industry.

However, together with the expansion of standardized testing has come a growing disenchantment with what many see as the dehumanization of education. In recent years, even the test publishers have been playing around with the possibility of a limited return to essay testing. But large-scale professional essay testing is different from the usual classroom essay test, and the two will be dealt with separately.

THE CLASSROOM ESSAY TEST

In most classroom essay tests, there are built-in ambiguities, both in the questions themselves and in the grading variations. As a result, no one set of advice will help you cope with the variety of question types and teacher expectations. But there are some general rules that you can use, working down from the *top* (that is, the unlikely situation in which you really know the answers to the questions) to the *bottom* (where you sit with glazed eyes, repenting all those great nights at parties when you should have been studying).

First of all, let's recognize the fact that essay answers are tremendously plastic. They can be stretched and pulled, expanded and condensed, skewed and twisted to meet the special circumstances with which you come to the test. And as they're given in many classrooms, essay tests beg for bull. Experienced test-takers have long recognized that there are effective ways of coping. In *Examining in Harvard College* (1963), William G. Perry wrote:

> *"But, sir, I don't think I really deserve it. It was mostly bull, really." This disclaimer from a student whose examinations we have awarded a straight "A" is wondrously depressing. Alfred North Whitehead invented its only possible rejoinder: "Yes sir, what you wrote is nonsense, utter nonsense. But ah! Sir! It's the right kind of nonsense!"*

The trick, then, is to find the right kind of nonsense.

General rules. Some rules apply to all essay questions. Many of them are the same ones that you've been reading in the chapter on general strategies:
- Know your teacher. This knowledge helps you to define the limits of credibility (in other words, to know how much bull you can sling).
- Read the question carefully.
- Know what you're asked to do; circle key words and terms.

140

- Be sure to answer all parts of the question, or as many parts as you have to answer for full credit.
- Write (on the back of the paper, or on scrap) the major facts, ideas, and formulas that are suggested as you read the question. Do this *before* you start to answer the question, and refer to this list as you go along to be sure you haven't left out some vital information. Do this for every question you intend to answer, before you start to write any of your answers; this will freeze your ideas for reference later, after you've become involved in the answer to a specific question. As a new idea comes to your mind during the writing of an answer, jot it down with the others so that you'll have it ready to fit in where it's needed.
- Organize the ideas, facts, and formulas in the order in which you intend to use them, by writing a number in front of each. Cross them out as you use them in your writing.

Identification questions. These aren't really essays except in the loosest sense of the word; but some teachers think that paragraph writing is a more efficient way of testing your ability to memorize information than answering objective questions. Besides, it's much easier to make up an identification test.

Identifications aren't bad if you organize your answer to parade what you know, to generalize what you're not sure of, and to gloss over what you don't know at all, implying that you know much more than you do. Here's one pretty effective approach:

- Identify the person or object by name.
- Give a category into which the person or object fits.
- Date it; if you don't have a specific date, approximate one.
- Provide at least one reason why he/she/it is important enough to be asked about.
- Try to fit in that one bit of information you know about him/her/it to suggest that you know much more than you're telling. Let's see how this works:

Identify Metternich.

Prince Metternich [if you remember that his first name was Klemens, you just made an extra point], an *Austrian statesman,* was *the leader of the reactionary forces* in Europe *following the defeat of Napoleon.* His major purpose *was to undo the work of the French Revolution and restore the Old Regime.* The period is sometimes called *The Age of Metternich.*

The last comment, of course, is not really part of the identification of Metternich. But it's the extra little bit of information that lets the reader know there's much more you could tell if you had the time. If you can answer the question *without* this kind of stretching, leave it out—especially if it isn't directly applicable. But it's a great cover for something you left out.

But suppose you don't have all the information at hand. Like a good cook, you make do with what you have, and stretch your ingredients. For example:

Identify the Yalta Conference.

The Yalta Conference was *a meeting held during World War II* of the *leaders of the Allied powers.* [You've just used up all that you remember about the Yalta Conference. In fact, you've already begun to stretch because you don't remember whether *all* the Allied leaders were there, or just the Big Three.] *Agreements were made on issues of the war and of the peace to follow.* [Sounds reasonable: it must have been one or the other or—with any kind of luck—both.] *It had profound effects on the postwar world.* [Why else would it be on the exam? Besides, even if you're off-base, you aren't actually *wrong*— just mistaken in judgment.]

If you're really desperate, you might go for broke and write: "Roosevelt became ill from the food served at Yalta." This is the kind of (mis)information that's almost impossible to pin down. Your teacher might write that he couldn't find any such evidence or that it's irrelevant. But you haven't lost anything. A word of caution: don't write a statement that can be proven false ("Stalin promised to hold free elections in the countries occupied by the Soviet Union").

Of course, there is the possibility that you've got the kind of teacher or professor who snarls, "That's not what I wanted." If you have identified your instructor as a member of the mind-reading class of testing, you'll have to use your class notes as a basis for identifying the *key phrases* and *significant comments* that this teacher has identified with a grasp of the subject. This approach will be necessary for all of the tests given by this kind of teacher.

Essay questions. The true essay question asks you to do something other than just identify a person or place or thing. One of your first tasks will be to figure out just how much precision the teacher is asking for. If you are just asked to "Discuss the role of monarchs in the rise of the nation-states of Europe," then you know that the teacher hasn't used the imperative verb with any sense of precision and is asking you to do one of two things: throw the bull, or guess what he has in mind. A lot of teachers and professors will tell you that they want brevity and quality rather than quantity. For the most part, take this admonition with a few grains of salt; most instructors are keenly aware of the amount of blue book you've used up. And when you're asked to "discuss *fully,*" you're being asked to write a Ph.D. dissertation (piled higher and deeper).

Besides, if you don't know anything about a subject and write nothing, you'll get no credit. On the other hand, after wading through four or five pages of even miscellaneous rambling on a topic, most readers figure that you've got to know *something,* and you'll most likely get *some* credit. One expert points out that one of the reasons for low validity of essay tests is the fact that most individuals get credit for writing, period, even if they have nothing to say.

If the question is fuzzy, then no matter how it's stated, you're really just being asked to "deal with" the subject at hand. (Just what does *discuss* mean?) Your task is to state and develop a thesis—a consistent and logical argument that runs through the discussion. Here are the steps:

Write a clearly stated introduction in which you present your thesis or theme.

• If the question is direct, begin with a direct answer. Don't repeat the whole question; most readers recognize this as an obvious space-filling ploy. On the other hand, pick up the key words in the question to show that you're starting a direct response to what is asked of you. For example:

> *Joseph Conrad said that* Victory *was more filled with "life stuff" than anything he had yet written. To what extent was this "life stuff" Conrad's own?*

> *Answer*: The "life stuff" in *Victory* is largely Conrad's own in that the personality of Alex Heyst reflects Conrad's own inability to relate with warmth to other human beings. . . .

• If the question is vague, you'll have to decide on your thesis or theme, and then start with a statement in which you express it. For example:

> *Discuss the place of traditional values in Hemingway's novels.*

> *Answer*: To Hemingway, self-discipline, not abstract qualities, is the mark of the hero.

Some people have trouble starting off because they can't pull a theme on which to focus. You might be surprised how few reference points you'll need that will apply to essays in a wide variety of subjects. A few starting points are:

Conflict:	Man's struggle against man (or machine, or the gods, or nature, or himself, or fate, or . . .)
Search:	Man's search for love (values, meaning, God, or . . .)
Symbolism:	Abstract concepts are illustrated by nature (persons, pictures, music, gestures, things, or . . .)
Love:	Man's love of his fellow man (woman, children, God, his dog, or . . .)
Courage:	Man's ability to survive (persist, struggle, maintain his integrity, or . . .)
Resignation:	Man's acceptance of the world (his own nature, love, fate, or . . .)

All of these, of course, are great in literature. But with just a little imagination, you'll discover how quickly you can convert these basic ingredients into good starting points in history, political science, anthropology, psychology, economics—and a lot more. Remember, teachers are very impressed with *profundities,* especially if they think they can recognize one of their own ("As you said so eloquently in one of your lectures, . . .").

The body of your essay supports your thesis. Each paragraph should present an argument, a reason, or evidence to support one point. Even if the question doesn't ask for facts or examples, present them. How many? Normally, offer two facts or examples to support each point. In cases where the facts elude you, develop your argument as well as you can in their absence. Be as clear and precise about *that one fact you really know,* and as vague as possible about the one you're not really sure of. And tie them together, somehow, to suggest that what the reader sees is only a fragment of what you know. For example:

> The Hemingway hero is a man of action, not an intellectual or a thinker. He distrusts noble sentiments: but his acts are consistent with his sense of self-discipline. This basic quality is illustrated in *The Sun Also Rises* and *A Farewell to Arms.* [You haven't actually read these books, so you daren't say too much, but it's reasonable to assume that Hemingway's M.O. will be reflected in most of his works.] It is perhaps most clearly illustrated in *The Old Man and the Sea.* [Of course, because this is the one work of Hemingway that you actually read.] In this tale [you don't remember if it was a novel or a short story], the hero. . . .

And so on. Work on what you do know for all it's worth. Mention specifics and names (but be sure you know how to spell them if you mention them). And pepper the essay with *key terms and phrases* and *theories* and *nuggets of wisdom* that your teacher or professor has mentioned during class lectures—if there's any way to fit them in without stretching the limits of relevance. This shows that you're relating what you learned in class with what you've read.

Most themes, rules, or generalizations do have exceptions—and mentioning exceptions helps establish your depth of knowledge and your grasp of the subject. But you don't want your reader to think that you've confused *examples* and *exceptions,* which brings us to another important rule: *label* everything you're doing. Write: "The basic rule is. . . ," "An example is. . . ," "An exception is. . . ," "On the other hand. . . ," "A comparable situation is. . . ." Don't ever expect the reader to figure out what you're doing, even if *you* think it's crystal clear.

The conclusion wraps up your thesis. You can reiterate your starting thesis, or you can expand it by citing corollaries, or you can paraphrase it. In effect, you'll follow the advice given a neophyte after-dinner speaker: "Tell 'em what you're going to say, say it, and tell 'em what you've said."

In most essay tests, examiners tend to be more impressed with a clearly defined organization and a logical development—as well as good grammatical writing—than with a firm grasp of the subject. *Well-developed* bull is frequently the key to "the right kind of nonsense." The essay test can be the joy of the obfuscator, who can often conceal his or her ignorance by a skillful display of organization and literary sleight-of-hand. In a letter-to-the-editor of *The Daily Princetonian* many years ago, writer Stephen Leacock wrote:

> *Every student should train himself to be like the conjurer Houdini. Tie him as you would, lock him in as you might, he got loose. A student should acquire this looseness. . . . There are a great number of methods of evasion. Much can be done by sheer illegibility of handwriting.*

But *be careful* here. Lots of instructors will *not* give you the benefit of the doubt if they can't make out what you wrote. So save scribbling for the moment of truth when you realize that doom is at hand and desperate measures are called for. In fact, if you *know* your stuff, write as legibly as possible. A number of studies show that the same answer will get a better grade if it's in good handwriting than if it's scribbled. Psychology professor N. M. Downie of Purdue tells of a young man who got hold of the required weekly papers of a student who had taken the same course with the same professor a year earlier; to cover up clues, he typed the papers (which had originally been handwritten)—and consistently got a letter grade higher on every paper.

Another moment of desperation may arise as you realize that the room is practically empty and you still have half of your test unfinished. The best advice here is to write, "Short of time. Please accept outline." And then do just what you promised: outline your answer. Present main points, subtopics, illustrations, examples, exceptions, ideas, arguments, and whatever, in good outline form. Many teachers are *willing* to give you the benefit of the doubt if you can present them with some reasonable evidence that you know what you're doing. And many *will* accept an outline as such evidence; after all, you've already demonstrated your ability to write in the earlier part of the test. (If you didn't, chances are you wouldn't have done any better at the end, either.) In any event, a good outline is far better than even a brilliant beginning that ends abruptly.

THE TAKE-HOME EXAM

Many students think this is a breeze. Don't kid yourself. Remember that your paper will be compared with that of the whiz kids and the pluggers in the class. So expect to make it long and complete, full of citations, references, and quotations.

Whatever you do, don't for a minute believe that *anybody* in the class is actually going to limit the time spent on the test to the three or four hours the prof suggested. If *you* accept his suggestion, you're aiming for the bottom of the normal distribution curve. In most ways, a take-home exam is tougher than a term paper. On your term report, the chances are that you chose your topic and treatment; but on the take-home exam, you're answering the same questions as Joe Grind, who's been working on it steadily for a week. You can rest assured that what Joe produces will be held against you.

Fortunately, the take-home exam has lost some of its popularity. The enthusiasm of teachers and professors ebbed as they recognized that the longer it takes to write a paper, the longer it takes to read it.

HOW WILL YOU BE GRADED?

The 1912 experiment of Starch and Elliot dramatized the wide range of grading techniques and standards used by teachers. Similar studies over the years reveal that the situation has changed remarkably little in over half a century. Just before World War II, a paper written by a journalist for a large metropolitan newspaper was submitted to 100 teachers, who were asked to grade it and estimate the grade level of the writer. The grades ranged from 60 to 98, and the estimates from fifth grade to a college junior! Furthermore, a number of studies have demonstrated that an answer in good handwriting will generally get at least one letter grade higher than the same answer in poor handwriting; so if your writing is particularly bad, a crash course in penmanship might be worth considering.

In *The Journal of Experimental Education* one experimenter reported that:

- the passing or failing of about 40% of students depends not on what they know or don't know, but on *who* reads their papers;
- the passing or failing of 10% of the papers depends on the time of day the papers are read; and
- the grade a paper gets is heavily influenced by the quality of the paper the grader read just before it. If a C paper is read after an A paper, it will probably drop to D, but if it is read after an F paper, it will likely rise to B. (So try not to hand in your test after one of the class bright lights; get right behind Geraldine Goof-Up.)

A lot of different systems get mixed up in determining the specific grade you'll get on your essay. For example, does the teacher deliberately "grade on the curve"? If so, then your mark will be determined as much by what your *classmates* do as by what *you* do. Does your teacher count only ideas? Or does he or she consider style? Neatness? Grammar and spelling? Form and procedure? Grades on essays reflect arbitrary criteria and the individual value systems of teachers. And how well the teacher enjoyed lunch, and whether he or she likes you as a person.

What makes the system particularly troublesome is that many teachers never make it clear in advance just what they expect and just what their standards are. This doesn't necessarily mean they're nasty: a lot of them have never clarified their standards in their own minds. This is why so many essay tests are returned with just grades, or with such immortal gems of diagnosis and advice as "Try harder!"

Some teachers are confused about the distinction between their obligation to evaluate your work on the basis of clearly defined standards and their right to express judgments about you and your work on the basis of whim. College professors, especially, often view as an infringement of their academic freedom any demands that they make their standards clear and then conform to them. As one observer puts it, classroom tests are "essentially private matters," known to the teacher, the students, and God. It's put a little differently by N. M. Downie in his book, *Fundamentals of Measurement*: "A basic reason for a large part of the unreliability [of essay tests] is that the typical reader of essay tests considers himself a final authority . . . [who] feels no need of any statistician or psychologist to help him do a job that he knows he is doing well."

It's interesting that prospective teachers get very little training in the grading of essay papers. That's too bad, because the experience of ETS shows that the reliability of essay grading (that is, the chances of different readers' giving you the same grade for the same work) can be raised to as high as .84.

Many authorities suggest that there are some simple ways in which essay grading can be made better and more objective. Anonymous grading, for example, can avoid bias and prejudice on the one hand, and the "halo effect" on the other; and it can be achieved in a variety of ways, such as by assigning numbers to be marked on the blue books instead of names. Some teachers set up clear criteria for grading. They take their own tests and establish checklists of all the possible correct answers they can think of. If the question called for two examples, then *any* two on the list will provide full credit (as far as *ideas* are concerned, anyhow). As they grade their papers, one question at a time, they add to the checklists correct answers they hadn't anticipated. In fact, some teachers actually distribute their checklists with the graded exam papers. Says one Chicago high school teacher, "It helps me as well as the kids. I always used to get arguments and feel resentment from the kids who thought I marked them unfairly. Now, if I ask for two examples, and they get back a checklist with a dozen possibilities, I don't get any hassles. They know exactly what I want, and the basis for the grades I give. It's worth the effort and time involved just to stop the fighting after every test."

Of course, there are some teachers (more of them in the colleges than in the high schools) who use the same moth-eaten tests year after year. They don't want anybody seeing the questions on their Basic Examination, or learning their basis for grading. (Someone described one such teacher who claimed to have had 20 years' experience as really having had one year's experience—repeated 20 times.)

The process of setting grading standards by committee (as do some high schools in New York when grading the State Regents Examination) has encouraged the notion of establishing clearly defined marking standards. But given the slow pace of educational reform (that mortarboard hat you'll wear at graduation was used as a writing desk by medieval students who sat on benches), it may be a long time before such standards are used to grade most essay tests.

THE STANDARDIZED ESSAY TEST

In Britain, essay tests traditionally have been accorded greater respect than objective tests. (The British played around with standardized objective tests for a while, largely as a result of American influence. But now such tests are used mainly for diagnosing reading problems for students who are failing.) To the British, essays are the best way to ascertain what students know and how they think. Almost half a century ago the standard was set for the national General Certificate of Education (GCE) exam; five teachers were to read each paper quickly for a general impression, and grade it. It was found that the average grades were very similar to the average grades of other groups of five teachers asked to mark the same paper. This system worked for many years, to the general satisfaction of English teachers and psychologists. But paying five teachers to read each paper is expensive, and the system has gradually eroded. In many European systems,

147

however, it is still traditional to have at least two teachers read each paper, with a third called in if the grades are too far apart. (By contrast, even in New York State, where committees often set up specific standards for each question on the Regents exam, only one teacher grades each question.)

In this country, psychometricians have pushed consistently for the abolition of the "unscientific" and unreliable essay exam. They point out the limited sampling of knowledge and behavior that can be measured in a handful of questions. They point to the element of luck in which a student may draw topics about which he or she knows a good deal—or may hit the one or two weak spots. And, they argue, objective tests of English writing ability predict grades in English composition courses better than do essays.

Teachers, on the other hand, argue that essay tests measure skills and abilities that simply cannot be measured by objective tests, such as the ability to develop original ideas, organize them in meaningful patterns, and express them in the test-taker's own words, without cues or prompting. Some agree with Marshall McLuhan, who thinks that the *way* an idea is expressed is as important as the idea itself.

The ups and downs of essay testing in standardized exam programs in this country reflect the maneuverings, skirmishes, and victories in the battles between the two groups. Shortly after World War II the psychometricians at ETS won a brief victory after submitting evidence that their objective verbal aptitude test could actually predict the ability to get good marks on compositions better than essays could. The essay tests were dropped from the ETS testing program.

English teachers protested, and reluctantly the ETS reintroduced a General Composition Test. This test, like the earlier essay test, was graded quite differently from the British tests. The American test-makers called for "scientific" grading procedures. The papers were graded by carefully prepared readers who spent three days in conference and training to ensure uniformity of standards and rules. The grades given by one reader correlated with those of another reader at about .70. This isn't bad for an essay, but it's much lower than the grading reliability of an objective test, in which the grade doesn't depend on who does the grading. Again the ETS psychometricians argued that the job could be done faster, cheaper, and more efficiently by machine-scoring of objective tests.

Again ETS dropped essay sections, and again English teachers reacted in horror. This time ETS decided on a compromise. Essay questions were asked, and the answers (called simply "writing samples") were sent out—ungraded—to the colleges to do with as they pleased.

In the meantime, ETS psychometricians rallied again to prove the unreliability of essay grading. In one experiment, 300 short essays written by college freshmen (the topics were "Who Should Go to College?" and "When Should Teen-Agers Be Treated as Adults?") were given to 53 teachers, editors, lawyers, business executives, social scientists, and natural scientists. The readers were asked to give each paper one of nine grades. The average correlation was .31. The correlation between the grades given by the English teachers, by the way, was an underwhelming .41. Analyzing the results, Dr. John W. French of ETS

148

admitted at a conference on testing problems that the objective tests did miss such qualities as form, flavor, and ideas. He added, wryly:

> *But, then, of course, they are also pretty much missed by the readers. The low correlations among the readers and the 101 papers receiving all nine grades can only mean that nothing at all is being measured very well by the essays. . . . In fact, the* well-trained *reader may simply be measuring verbal aptitude—poorly.*

Nevertheless, continuing pressure for an essay section persuaded ETS, in 1977, to reintroduce an essay section on the English Composition Test. The 20-minute essay was accompanied by 40 minutes of multiple-choice questions designed to measure "the student's ability to do the kind of writing required in most college courses."

The grading system of the current essay comes close to that of the British system. Readers gather for five days of "a reading," working together to set standards. Groups of eight readers work together under the leadership of a chief reader who periodically presents samples to the group to ensure uniformity of standards. Each essay is read by three readers.

However, the essays are read "holistically." That means that no attempt is made to judge each quality separately. Readers are instructed to read essays quickly and judge them as a whole. The grades range from 1 (the lowest) to 4 (the highest), and no reader knows the score another reader has given the essay. The scale of 1 to 4 is designed to prevent the giving of middle, or uncommitted scores. The total score on the essay is the sum of the scores given by the three readers. But the score reported out is the combined score of the essay part and the multiple-choice part, so you won't get a subscore for the essay.

There are some major differences between essay tests given in subject classrooms and essay tests given as part of a standardized test (optional essays are also given in ETS achievement tests, and there is a new optional English Composition Test in the CLEP series). In order to achieve the relatively high correlation between readers, something had to be sacrificed on the standardized essay test. That something, generally, is in the area of *ideas* and *subject knowledge.* In other words, most of the essays given on national exams focus on *mechanics* and *wording.* Because these are the major concerns of the objective tests in English, the ETS essay tests will really measure the same qualities as its short-answer *Test of Standard Written English*—but, according to ETS psychometricians, not as well.

So if you're taking an essay test on a general aptitude test (like verbal ability or English composition) worry more about form, mechanics, grammar, spelling, and flow than about profundity of ideas or about showing off how *much* you know. It's how *well* you write, not *what* you write that counts.

The fight between the teachers and the psychometricians goes on. The question of whether you'll have an essay test in your next aptitude battery will depend on who seems to be winning the fight at the time. But given the fact that such essay tests seem to be measuring pretty much the same qualities as the short-answer tests, it won't make a great deal of difference.

Afterword
Trends in Tests and Test-Taking

Of course, tests are necessary in American schools and industry. Applying what you've learned is proof that you've learned it. But in the past, the test of most learning has been in the student's actual *behavior*. (If primitive hunters had not learned to hunt, they would "fail"—and starve.) Now, formal school testing has moved from the realm of actual performance to a kind of middle activity—taking paper-and-pencil exams from which we infer that students have learned what they were supposed to. But over the years, it has also become pretty apparent that success in this middle activity doesn't correlate very well with success in actual performance. At the same time that testing and test-taking have mushroomed in America, some test designers, test givers, and test-takers have become increasingly concerned about the discrepancies between most schools' and organizations' professed objectives and the tests that are used to measure the achievement of these objectives. Some trends are emerging that may influence the shape of testing and test-taking in the future.

150

HOW ARE TESTS CHANGING?

A very small group of test designers and critics has begun to go beyond mere criticism of tests to the creation of different kinds of testing. These critics have built on proposals developed over the past three decades to design tests that more nearly measure what they purport to measure.

Spearheading the drive toward reform in recent years has been the formulation by test experts Benjamin Bloom and David Kratwohl of a *taxonomy*, or classification system, of intellectual abilities. Bloom and Kratwohl were engaged in writing examinations at the University of Chicago shortly after World War II. They were impressed with the difficulties they encountered in developing test questions that actually measured success in the achievement of the goals and objectives listed for the courses. At the heart of the problem, they thought, was the fact that the course objectives were simply too vague to be measurable. (How does one measure "appreciation" or "understanding" or "critical thinking"?) And so they developed a classification of cognitive, or thinking, skills. At the bottom of their hierarchy they identified *knowledge*, which they defined as simply *knowing* things. (This ranking becomes significant when it is recognized that knowledge is the level at which most school tests are geared.) Beyond the skill of simply knowing or remembering, they categorized a number of cognitive skills and abilities, including:

• *Comprehension*, or understanding. Aspects of comprehension include the ability to *translate*, or express a communication in a form different from that in which it was received; to *interpret*, or explain a communication in terms of the relationship of ideas, and to *extrapolate*, or project and predict from given data.

• *Application*, or the ability to use appropriate abstractions or principles and rules in specific situations.

• *Analysis*, or the ability to identify the component parts of a communication.

• *Synthesis*, or the ability to put elements and parts together to form a new and consistent whole—this is the basis of creativity.

• *Evaluation*, or the ability to apply clearly defined standards in assessing items and in making value judgments.

The taxonomy developed by Bloom and Kratwohl, together with recommendations such as those proposed in the 1950's by the American Council on Education's Cooperative Study of Evaluation in General Education, has become the basis for a whole set of testing standards. If knowledge is to be *de*emphasized in testing, then students are given information they are expected to *do* something with—to demonstrate that they understand it, can analyze it, or interpret it, or apply it to specific situations. While the ability to remember is important, it should not take precedence over the higher abilities that we profess to emphasize.

The basic principle here is that students should be permitted to do what lawyers, historians, and scientists do in their work: refer to information when they need it to comprehend, apply, analyze, synthesize, or evaluate. And like historians, lawyers, and scientists, if students use information frequently enough, they will find they come to "know" it without having to look it up every time.

Such reform proposals have had some impact, mostly on standardized tests. So far, the results in the area of classroom tests have been spotty and almost imperceptible.

One promising direction in testing is teachers' increasing awareness that norm-referenced tests don't give any real guidance for curriculum design or the improvement of instruction, or even the diagnosis of problems. They provide no real goals or targets.

Indeed, part of the fuzziness that surrounds the purpose of testing in our schools is the fact that most tests—including the widely used standardized tests—*are* norm-referenced. They're used to compare a student's achievement in math or English or history or biology against an *average* based on the achievement of a group: a class population, a school population, or a national population. Therefore, an A− means only that the student did better on the test than the student who received a C+. It really doesn't tell much about what the A student *understands* about math, English, history, or biology. And norm-referenced tests don't tell us what the C+ student *doesn't* understand. For example, we don't know *why* SAT scores have been declining in recent years; and we don't know what to do about it. The only function such tests are really well suited for is to categorize, cull, classify—and to predict in terms of these same classifications. They don't do this badly because they help to create the very categories they predict.

All norm-referenced tests are based on the principle that no matter how good or bad schooling is, half the population will be "above normal" and half will be "below normal." *Relative improvement for any individual is always at the expense of somebody else.* For large parts of our population, the message is: you can never do well; you're one of life's born losers. If an extremely high correlation exists between IQ and school grades, this means, in effect, that schools grade students not on the results of *instruction,* but on abilities and aptitudes that those students had before they even walked into the classrooms.

The growing awareness of the deficiencies of norm-referenced tests has pushed some test experts in an interesting new direction: *criterion-referenced* testing. Criterion-referenced tests are based on the identification of specific educational objectives expressed in clearly observable and measurable competencies, rather than on comparative rankings of poorly defined "understandings." Such tests can tell us which of a series of clearly defined tasks a student can or cannot achieve. We have a way of knowing the results of school instruction; we can determine whether instruction and curriculum have been successful in accomplishing specific objectives.

Professor W. James Popham of UCLA, a leader in the area of criterion-referenced testing, defines six criteria for good criterion-referenced tests:

- An unambiguous descriptive scheme [just what skills are measured?]
- An adequate number of items to measure each specified behavior
- A sufficiently limited focus
- Reliability
- Validity
- Strangely enough, normative data. While it is important to identify where

a student stands on the scale of competencies, Popham thinks, it is equally important to evaluate his achievement in terms of his peers' achievements.

The major difference between the two types, say critics, is that the normative data are subordinated in criterion-referenced testing. And some researchers claim that if we forget about that normal curve of distribution, we can get *most* students to achieve at mastery levels that are now considered achievable only by A students. The work done by a number of investigators has convinced such scholars as Benjamin Bloom that as students go through school, the schools have contributed to the widening of the normal curve because we assume that half the population *must* do poorly, and we do little about failure. The definition of *aptitude* as a given volume of *ability* (either innate or learned) presupposes a continuation of that spread. But consider the curriculum and instructional changes that would be inevitable if we accept John B. Carroll's definition of aptitude as the *time* it takes for a student to learn a given competency. In this case, we would no longer take the time and the instruction as fixed, but as possible variables, with progression through the levels of mastery as our goal for all our students. It means a whole new curriculum scale, with divisions into learning units by task or competency, not into blocks of time called terms or grades. It means that students could progress at their own speeds through a manageable, well-defined, clearly organized curriculum based on specified tasks whose achievement can be measured with precision.

Some schools are based on these principles, but not many. Even with all the criticism of norm-referenced tests, they'll be around for a long time. For one thing, if *most* students achieve the competencies that the schools claim to teach, how will we know who is "better"? For another, school board members and administrators need someone to tell them how one school system stacks up against another. And much of the public needs some simpleminded standards by which to tell if schools are "good" or "bad."

But the increased interest in criterion-referenced testing is a hopeful sign of eventual change. A lot of teachers are talking about it, and even producing criterion-referenced tests. Most of those made up in schools are still not very good, but at least the focus in these schools has begun to move away from just comparing students. And with time and training, such tests should improve.

TESTING AND STUDENT PRIVACY

School success or failure is determined in large part by test scores. And especially for very young schoolchildren, school and society mean almost the same thing. Self-images and aspirations for the future are created in the early years. And success or failure in schools are publicized to degrees that would be considered intolerable in almost any other area of our society.

Increasingly, community and political leaders (reforms in education rarely come from within the schools) have begun to ask questions about students' rights to keep private their own successes or failure. The Buckley-Pell amendment to the General Educational Provisions Act of 1974 has done much to protect students' rights to privacy. The Department of Health, Education and Welfare has made it clear that students and parents may have access to records that directly involve students, and that outsiders have no right to such information without the consent of the students or their parents. But there's still a long way to go. Many schools and colleges still routinely violate the spirit of the Buckley-Pell amendment. Professor Clinton I. Chase, director of the Bureau of Educational Studies and Testing at Indiana University, points to some of the major violations:

• *Calling for a show of hands on test grades.* Teachers often want to know the score distribution on a test, or how many students got a particular question right or wrong. They may want to do an "item analysis"—that is, to know how well a test question "discriminates" between high and low scorers. But such work is laborious and time-consuming. So ETS, in a booklet entitled *Short-Cut Statistics for Teacher-Made Tests,* informs teachers that "all this work can be done by a show of hands in class in so little time that students do not resent it." If they don't, they should. How many teachers would be willing to reveal to groups of peers and colleagues their own shortcomings and failures by a show of hands demanded by an administrator?

• *Students marking other students' papers.*

• *Students sorting out their own papers from a class pile.* Teachers and professors frequently are reluctant to take the time to arrange and pass out scored test papers. Often students are invited to sort through everybody's business in getting to their own papers. This may be a great ego boost to the A students; how about those who didn't do well?

• *Posting class rosters with test scores.* This is a common practice in many schools and colleges, especially after the final exam. It's also a violation of your right to keep your business to yourself. Some schools have been persuaded to assign numbers to students, so that names don't appear publicly with grades.

Many well-meaning teachers engage in such abridgements of students' rights to privacy simply because they have never thought much about the matter, or because "that's the way it's always been done." If you object, you might bring the matter to the attention of your teacher or professor as tactfully as possible. Increasingly, schools and teachers are becoming more sensitive to their professional responsibilities in the matter of respecting students' rights. In many cases, student and parent pressures have played a major role in promoting such sensitivity.

LEARNING HOW TO TAKE TESTS

At the same time that the use of standardized tests in this country is growing, the criticism of such testing is also mounting. Despite the call for a moratorium on standardized testing from such organizations as the National Education Association, it isn't likely that the use of such tests will slow down. But the criticism is bringing about a growing recognition that test-taking has become a major academic skill that the schools have ignored. Increasing numbers of school administrators, teachers, parents, and students are awakening to the fact that test-taking skills can be learned in intelligently planned long-range programs. Few programs have gone as far as that of Washington, D.C., whose associate super-intendent of instruction said, "We want all our students to do well. [We'll] even begin to tell them some of the things on the test." Nevertheless, more and more Americans have come to recognize that understanding a subject doesn't guarantee doing well on tests.

One result is a growing interest in tests by parents and test-takers. After all, these tests will play a major role in shaping the future of young Americans, many of whom are woefully ignorant of test-making and test-taking. But then, so are many teachers. A fascinating set of contradictions governs the traditional Ameri-can view of test-making. On the one hand, college professors of history, physics, French, or math scorn instruction in test-making, on the ground that one needs only to know history, physics, French, or math in order to test students in those subjects. For a professor of an academic subject to learn something about teaching or testing is considered somehow demeaning. On the other hand, a knowledge of test-making is deemed by psychometricians to be so difficult to grasp that laymen had best not attempt to make tests, which should be constructed and discussed only by experts who have devoted their lives to the study of the mysteries involved! Outsiders are kept away by a number of devices, including the use of an arcane language (a test-maker with his or her professional costume on is a "psycho-metrician," for example). The fact is that, while some of the manipulations may be quite complicated, the basic ideas are really simple and understandable. (You might want to go back to Chapter 3, to learn something about test-making, so that you, too, can talk glibly of "coefficients of predictive validity.")

Oscar Buros, sometimes called the Ralph Nader of testing, has probably done more than any other individual to make tests intelligible to those who buy them, use them, and take them. His prestigious *Mental Measurements Yearbooks* contain reviews of hundreds of standardized tests by experts in the field. And yet it's amazing how many school administrators and teachers don't check these reviews before they buy or administer tests that will shape their students' futures. In recent years, students and parents in some communities have begun to refer to Buros' *Yearbooks,* and to keep check on the quality of the tests used in their communities.

Another result of the recognition that test-taking is a skill is the increased interest in coaching courses and training programs which—like the tests them-selves—range from quite good to very bad. In January 1977, Jerrold Zacharias of M.I.T., an outspoken critic of standardized testing, told a senior editor of *The American School Board Journal*:

> *I don't think any line can be drawn between legitimate test-taking preparation and inappropriate coaching. A test should be worth teaching to. If the tests are any good, then preparing children to take them is a perfectly sound educa-tional activity. Unfortunately, in the present case, the tests are terrible—intellectually reprehensible.*
>
> *Still, if you're going to be involved with these tests, it would be stupid not to engage in test-taking instruction.*

155

Many of the tests given in schools and industry are bad. Most of them are irrelevant to their professed purposes; they are far better for classifying people than for helping them. By and large, most schools in the past have had no incentive to teach test-taking. They are committed to the normative notion that half of the students will do well and half poorly. No matter what schools do or don't do, the normal curve within a district will remain fairly constant on a norm-referenced basis—unless the schools engage in revolutionary rethinking of goals and objectives.

More and more school administrators and teachers have begun to worry because, in recent years, more and more schools and school districts are being compared *against each other*. Increasing numbers of schools have begun to think of teaching test-taking. But although schools and colleges are the major test administrators, teachers don't know much about test-taking skills. The teachers will have to learn this subject, just as you will.

If you are committed to learning test-taking, you can do it. But you'll have to give it at least the same commitment and effort that you give to learning any major skill. In the long run, the effort you apply to learning test-taking will pay off far more handsomely than the effort to learn most school subjects. Your future depends on your skill in taking tests. True reform in testing appears a long way off, and in the foreseeable future, truly skilled test-takers should be able to continue to beat the system.

Index

Index

Cherokee "syllabary," 17
Chicago Test of Primary Mental Abilities, 24–25
"Chitling test," 11, 12
Classroom essay test, 140–45
Classroom tests, 55–68
Cleary, T. Anne, 10
Clifford, Paul I., 76
Coaching, as means of raising scores, 77–79
College Boards, 69, 74, 79–80
  See also, SAT
College Characteristic Handbook, 76
College English Placement Exam, 43
College Entrance Examination Board (CEEB), 76, 78
College Level Examination Program (CLEP), 41, 85–88, 149
Competencies, 30
Completion tests, 56–57
Comprehending in reading, 17
Content validity, 38
Criterion-referenced evaluation, 30
Curve, 31–34

Dawes, Robyn M., 77
Dear, Robert E., 77–78
Decoding in reading, 16–17
Department of Health, Education and Welfare, 154
Deviation, 37
Diagnostic tests, 72–73
Dove, Adrian, 11
Dove Counterbalance General Intelligence Test, 12
Downie, N.M., 145, 146
Dyer, Henry, 4, 15, 16

Ebel, Robert L., 15, 38
Educational and Psychological Measurement, 75
Educational Testing Service (ETS), 15, 16, 38, 53, 69, 70, 71, 78, 146, 148, 149, 154
Einstein College of Medicine, 21, 23
Elliot, Edward, 139, 145
Englemann, Siegfried, 20, 21
English Composition Test, 149
English Usage Test, 82
Essay examination, 138–49
Evaluation, 29–31

Evans, Franklin R., 78
Examining in Harvard College, 140

Face validity, 38
Fishman, Joshua A., 76
Florida Atlantic University, 86
French, John W., 16, 41, 43, 77–78, 148–49
Fundamentals of Measurement (Downie), 146

"g" factor, 24, 25
General Certificate of Education (GCE), 147–48
General Composition Test, 148
General Educational Provisions Act of 1974, 153–54
General Examinations, CLEP, 85–86, 87
Ghetto Soul Test, 12
Goddard, Henry, 11
Graduate Record Exam (GRE), 10, 23, 39, 76–77, 79, 80–82
Grammar and usage skills, improvement of, 119–22
Grammar and usage tests, 111–17
Graph and chart reading tests, 131–37
Griggs vs. The Duke Power Company, 5
Griswold, A. Whitney, 138
Gross, Richard E., 3
Guessing, 48–49
Guilford, J.P., 24, 73–74
Guines, James, 78
Guion, Robert, 5–6

Handbook on Formative and Summative Evaluation of Student Learning, 73
Harcourt Brace Jovanovich, 15
Harrington, Michael, 70
Hawkes, Herbert E., 58
Heber, Rick, 20
Henmon-Nelson tests, 24
Herrnstein, R.J., 9
"Hidden curriculum," tests as, 2–3
Hoepfner, Ralph, 39
Hoffman, Banesh, 3, 74–75, 138
Holt, John, 3, 20
How Children Fail (Holt), 3, 20

Intelligence, 9–10
IQ
  defined, 10–13
  raising, 21–24

Index

Recognition, 16
Reliability, 35, 36–37
Roberts, S.O., 79
Rosenthal, Robert, 2
Rudman, Masha, 47

Scholastic aptitude, 13
Scholastic Aptitude Test (SAT), 10, 11, 35, 39, 69, 70, 73, 75, 76, 77, 79–80, 82
SAT-M, 75
SAT-V, 75
Schools, The (Mayer), 19, 70–71
Self-fulfilling prophecy, 2
Sequoya, 17
Seyfarth, John T., 20
Short-Cut Statistics for Teacher-Made Tests, 154
Siegelman, Marvin, 75
Simon, Theodore, 10
Smith, Arthur E., 7, 71
Smith, John, 78
Social Studies Reading Test, 83
Spache, George D., 18
Speed reading, 18
Speed tests, 44
Spelling skills, improvement of, 117–19
Spelling tests, 110–11
SRA Primary Mental Abilities Test, 25
Standard deviation, 32
Standard error, 2, 37
Standardization, 35, 36
Standardization sample, 36
Standardized essay test, 147–49
Standardized tests, 35, 69–88
Stanford-Binet IQ test, 10, 11
Stanines, 32
Starch, Daniel, 139, 145
Student Profile Report, 82
Suffixes, 105–8

Teaching as a Subversive Activity (Postman and Weingartner), 3
Terman, Lewis, 10–11, 13
Test of Standard Written English, 149
Test-makers, figuring intent of, 49–50
Test-making, 29–39
Test Service Bulletin #45 (Psychological Corporation), 74
Test-taking
strategies of, 40–54
trends, 150–56

Tests
achievement, 73
classroom, 55–68
classroom essay, 140–45
completion, 56–57
diagnostic, 72–73
essay, 138–49
grammar and usage, 111–17
graph and chart reading, 131–37
IQ, 35
matching questions, 60–62
multiple-choice, 62–68
numerical ability, 123–37
Numerical series, 128–31
predictive, 73–77
power, 44
speed, 44
spelling, 110–11
standardized, 35, 69–88
standardized essay, 147–49
true-false, 57–60
verbal aptitude, 89–108
writing ability, 109–22
Tests in Print (Buros), 7–8
True score, 37
True-false tests, 57–60
Turnbull, William, 15, 69, 71
Tyranny of Testing, The (Hoffman), 138

Underachiever, 14–15
University of Wisconsin, 75
USAFI, 87

"Vaccination theory of education," 3
Validity, 35, 37–39
Verbal analogies, 99–103
Verbal aptitude tests, 89–108
Vocabulary tests, 91–95

Washburn, S. L., 7
Weingartner, Charles, 3
Whimbey, Arthur, 21, 22–23
Wilcox, Lee, 75
Williams, Robert L., 1, 11, 14
Word meanings, 91–95
Writing ability skills, improvement of, 117–22
Writing ability tests, 109–22

Zacharias, Jerrold, 7, 155

160